DON'T TOUCH THAT DIAL!

First of all, check your own ratings

TEST NUMBER 1:

Twenty-five Questions About TV
You Probably Can't Answer If You're Under Thirty
*This one might help explain why your
parents are so weird.* (Chapter 5, page 95)

TEST NUMBER 2:

Twenty-five Questions About TV
You Probably Can't Answer If You're Over Forty
*Those kids love to make you feel hopelessly out of it —
here's some of the stuff that allows
them to do it.* (Chapter 5, page 98)

PLUS:

• The remote control gene that makes men and women different.
• Are you cable-ready or cable-impaired? This test might even help you
find the button on the remote.
• The highs and lows of famous careers. Did you spot them before they
made it big?

And Much, Much More!

The Ultimate Test of
TV TRIVIA

····· Jaime O'Neill ·····

HarperPaperbacks
A Division of HarperCollinsPublishers

HarperPaperbacks *A Division of* HarperCollins*Publishers*
10 East 53rd Street, New York, N.Y. 10022

Cover photographs courtesy of Archive Photos

Designed by Claudyne Bianco

First printing: February 1994

Printed in the United States of America

HarperPaperbacks and colophon are trademarks of HarperCollins*Publishers*

❖ 10 9 8 7 6 5 4 3 2 1

This book is dedicated to my mother and father,

Arthur and Evelyn O'Neill, of Welaka, Florida.

CONTENTS

Introduction: TV or No TV, These Are the Questions

"Television won't matter in your lifetime or mine."
REX LAMBERT, *The Listener*, 1936

"The only thing I like about television is its ephemerality."
P. J. O'ROURKE, 1987

I can still remember the very first image I ever saw on a television screen—a trumpet player in profile, fairly close up, the horn tilted skyward. This was in 1951. I was at my grandparents' house in rural Illinois. There is not much else I remember from 1951. For instance, I do not remember who that trumpet player was (if I ever knew) and I do not remember what tune he was playing. I do not remember what I ate for dinner that evening, nor do I remember what kind of car we rode in to get to my grandfather's house. I don't remember what my grandmother wore that day, or any other day in 1951.

But I remember the image of that trumpet player, a murky silhouette in tones of gray, and black, and white. The picture was "snowy." That was a word we used quite often back in those days. I never hear anyone say that anymore. The picture was so snowy, in fact, that we virtually had to assemble the image for ourselves, tracing the outline of the man's head and his trumpet, distinguishing the darker grays from the lighter grays until his shape emerged.

There couldn't have been more than a few thousand television sets in the whole state of Illinois on that day in 1951. (There were only about six million television sets in American homes at the beginning of 1951, though that year would see another sixteen million sold.) If you had one, you were suddenly very popular. My entire family—aunts, uncles, cousins, nephews—had assembled for the unveiling of my grandparents' new television set, a gathering that seldom took place even on holidays. There was a palpable sense of anticipation and excitement. My grandfather ran around the room with the "rabbit ears," a primitive indoor antenna that produced nearly indiscernible changes in picture quality. "There, Wilbur, right there, stand still," my grandmother would say, and my grandfather would lock himself in place, arms aloft, trying to snatch invisible signals out of the air.

For a long time there was nothing much to see or hear—a rush of static and electronic pulsations of light and dark. Still, we remained fixed to the set, the lot of us.

And then he materialized on the screen, called forth out of thin air, that trumpet player. My grandfather froze with the antenna, and my entire family let out a collective exclamation.

We didn't know it then—surely I didn't know it—but we had, at that moment, joined a larger family, a growing family of viewers whose lives would be shaped by these flickering and indistinct images, whose memories would be formed by what they saw on screens like the one we peered at so intently. What we would know of our times would come to us through this device—the wars, the assassinations, the social and political upheavals, the weighty and the trivial events, those near and those far away.

Except, of course, the very notion of what was near and what was far away had already begun to change.

More than forty years have passed since I saw the fuzzy image of that trumpet player. It is now as impossible to imagine a world *without* television as it would have been to imagine a world *with* television just a few short years before that day in 1951.

Perhaps you, too, remember the first image you ever saw on a television screen. Or, perhaps not. If you were born within the last forty years, you came into a world where television was already a central fact of life, so it was in the room even before your memories began to form. But there are television memories that go far back with you, too—the theme music from "Sesame Street," maybe. (Sure, you can call up the lyrics even as you are reading these words. "Sunny day, chasin' the _____ . . .") There are things you saw on television that are more firmly imprinted on your memory than things that happened to you in "real" life. There are characters from half-forgotten situation comedies whose names you recall, but you wouldn't remember the name of the clerk at the checkout counter of the market you've shopped at for years if she didn't wear a name tag. You don't claim to know much history, but if you're old enough, you remember the image of John-John Kennedy saluting the flag-draped coffin of his father, and you remember the image of Nixon giving that stiff wave as he boarded the helicopter on his last day in office. You you remember the Challenger explosion, and perhaps you remember where you were when you first saw that horrifying image. Or you remember the face of Anita Hill testifying before that bank of senators.

Like the songs we sung in high school, these images bring back the times of our lives; they remind us of who we were, how we were, the way we felt at those times. For good or ill, for better or worse, our lives are saturated with the images we've soaked up, year in and year out, through our television sets.

Much has been written about the power of television, and it's difficult to overstate that power. When Mount Saint Helens erupted in Washington state, it was one of the most awesome displays of nature's force a human being can witness. The entire top of a mountain blew off. People drove from great distances to witness the event, but at the site many of those people were to be found clustered around a news crew's television monitor, choosing to watch on a screen what was happening much more hugely and vividly right in front of them. Televised "reality" was, apparently, more "real" and more riveting than the event itself, unfiltered by the camera.

In a less dramatic way, I've seen the same phenomenon in my classrooms. For a time, I taught public speaking to college students. In order to give student speakers a sense of how they appeared to their audience, it was customary to videotape some of their speeches. If the monitor was facing the audience, the audience would, inevitably, watch the monitor while the student speaker was making his or her speech. Given the choice between watching flesh-and-blood reality or a reduced-sized, black-and-white, two-dimensional representation of that reality, people would, always, watch the screen, not the person. Finally, I had to turn the monitor so the audience could not see it while the speaker was giving a presentation. It was too distracting. The speaker could not make or maintain eye contact with the audience. They were glued to the tube.

That is a great power.

But none of us like to admit the power television has over us. When it comes to television, most of us are closet couch potatoes. In this country, you can go on a talk show and disclose just about anything about your personal life, but those of us at home are very slow to disclose the fact that we watch all that disclosure. After all, Americans are a robust, active, outdoor people. We don't squander our lives lying about, feeding our eyes with televised daydreams.

But, of course, we do.

An estimated 300 million people in over forty countries watched all or part of the 44th Emmy Awards in 1992. That's an awful lot of people in a world where it's hard to find anyone who will admit to watching much television. At that award ceremony, Candice Bergen facetiously thanked the vice president for his help in winning her an Emmy. That's a fairly high level of cultural significance. And if there was much on display at that ceremony honoring mediocrity, bad taste, and a bland sameness, then it is difficult to escape blame for raising all that to the level of such national importance. We watched the stuff, after all. We propelled these people to the heights of their stardom, laughed at the same recycled gags, thrilled to the same tired formulas.

Yet the fact of it is like a mountain—implacable, real, massive, and *there*. Even turning off the infernal machine won't make it go away because the print media now covers television coverage, and most small talk is fueled by what people have seen on TV. When the marines landed in Somalia, television made the landing, too. When President Bush threw up on the prime minister of Japan, television showed us that. When Jerry Seinfeld bet his friends that he could abstain from masturbating longer than they could, we were a party to the wager. Television news even took us into President Reagan's colon. Millions of people are more intimately involved in the lives of soap opera characters than they are in the lives of their friends and relatives. Personal tragedies are served up as made-for-TV movies, giving us the disease of the week, the murder of the week, the wacko of the week. Reality shows further blur the line between news and entertainment, between what is real and what is fictional. Children's programming is a vast marketing tool that creates characters primarily so that facsimiles of those characters can be sold to kids. For adults, advertising continues to exploit our insecurities and our desires to be accepted. Meanwhile, talk shows focus our attention on the bizarre, the titillating, and the tacky. Tabloid shows continue this obsession into the early prime-time hours with peep-show glimpses of life designed to hold us from commercial to commercial.

These are all familiar observations and lamentations, but are we not shaped by all of this? And if we are shaped by it, is it not better to be aware of what is shaping us, to take a moment or two to recollect what we've been watching?

Is there anything we've seen on television that is worth remembering? Perhaps not, but remember it we do. Or, more precisely, we remember bits and pieces of it. Like other memories, much of what we retain seems randomly selected—snatches of songs, characters from soaps or sitcoms, advertising slogans endlessly repeated until we had no choice but to store them in our memories. For at least two generations, the only reality the Korean War had was the reality represented by "M*A*S*H." For others, the entire civil rights movement of the 1960s is coalesced into Martin Luther King's "I Have a Dream" speech, rebroadcast several times each year.

As I began to compile the questions that make up this book, I became increasingly uncomfortable about how much I knew about so many silly, inconsequential, and even stupid things. In fact, if it's true that one's life flashes before one's eyes in the moments before death, I'm afraid a lot of my flashback is going to be reruns. Perhaps yours, too.

This book, then, is not a celebration of television; it is an acknowledgment of the *fact* of television, and the role it has played in our lives. Television may be ephemeral—series come and go, actors and actresses rise and fall, commercial products are hyped, then forgotten—but some of that flickering ephemerality leaves imprints behind. The repetition of slogans and jingles and theme songs records itself on our memories. Our memories are indiscriminate collectors, storing things we don't need while more important things slip away. The number of Americans who retain the image of Beaver Cleaver or remember the opening notes to "The Tonight Show" theme vastly outnumber the Americans who can cough up the name of their senator or congressman. Americans know of Matt Dillon, a fictional hero of the American West, but far fewer know of men like Bill Tilghman or a legion of other real-life western lawmen. Our political discourse can get very exercised about a fictional unwed mother and a baby that doesn't exist while the plight of real single mothers is virtually ignored in the formation of public policy. Whatever television reality is, it has gone a long way toward supplanting or superseding real "reality," whatever that might be in the fortysomething year of the television age.

Like most people, I harbor the deep suspicion that all this is probably not good for me, that it is doing things to my perception of the world that are not good for me, physically, psychically, emotionally, and intellectually. You would be hard-pressed to find anyone in this country who would claim they were better—by any definition of "better"—because of the television they have watched. For whatever reason, most of us carry the suspicion that we have been diminished by all that time spent basking in the blue light. That amounts to a national schizophrenia. Since we watch so much television and feel so much vague guilt about that fact, we are living a daily contradiction.

Guilt notwithstanding, we are committed to television. According to a poll conducted by *TV Guide* in 1991, one in four Americans wouldn't give up television for a million dollars. Forty-six percent of those polled would give up television, but they wouldn't take less than a million to make the sacrifice. Sixty-three percent of us watch television while we eat. Among young people, that number is even higher—76 percent. Only 12 percent of those polled said they felt guilty about watching television. Denial: the disease of the decade.

Whether or not you feel guilty about all that time in front of the tube will determine part of your response to the questions in this book. Do you know the answers to most of the questions compiled here? What will the test results tell you about yourself? Probably not very much. If you do well on these tests, then it is surely probable that you've watched a good deal of television. If you do well on these tests, it is probable that you have a sound and retentive memory. More important than the test results, however, is how you feel about those test results. If you know most of the stuff in this book, and if you feel proud of that fact, then you're a pretty well-adjusted person, or so it seems to me. You do what you do, and you make no apologies for that.

But, if you've watched a lot of television, you've surely been the subject of other people's disdain, or their earnest efforts to improve you. Get more exercise, they say, or get a little fresh air. Why don't you do something with yourself? they say. Get a life, they say.

But television viewers do have a life. We can go to "Cheers," and they're always glad to see us. We've had our brief love affairs with Annette Funicello or Farrah Fawcett-Majors, Tom Selleck or Mark Harmon, and we have not felt the sting of their rejection. We've sipped wine with the Frugal Gourmet, and eaten foods unobtainable in our town at the table of Julia Child. We have ridden in cars we could never afford to drive, traveled to places we could never afford to go. We have traveled backward and forward in time—to the Middle Ages, the American frontier, and distant galaxies of the distant future.

This book is a test of that parallel life we've led, those places we've gone and people we've seen.

So, it's time for you to take on these questions, some obscure, some commonly known. Where have you been all your life? If you can answer most of these questions, you'll have some idea.

The Ultimate Test of TV Trivia: Instructions for Use

Before we begin, you'll need a few instructions. This thing you hold in your hand is called a "book." Perhaps you are familiar with this low-tech apparatus from your experience with *TV Guide*. If you know how to use a *TV Guide*, then using this book should not be too difficult; the principle for operation is much the same.

First, you'll notice that this book technology does not come with a remote-control device. Moving from place to place in a book is accomplished by turning the pages. This must be done manually.

Pages turn from right to left. If television technology has shortened your attention span, this method of advancing through the book will, at first, seem tedious. It is certainly archaic. You will be tempted to flip the pages. Flipping pages is usually accomplished through use of the thumb. Flipping pages is the book equivalent of channel surfing with your remote-control device. Unlike with television, however, this method will prove unsatisfactory. Each page of a book is made up of words. In order to decipher words and their messages, you must pause, linger, even think for a moment or two. That, in fact, is the main reason why this technology is no longer as popular as it once was.

You'll also be disappointed to find that books do not come with sound, unless you provide it yourself by reading aloud, or better still, having it read aloud to you. That method is, in fact, recommended for this book, since it is largely made up of questions. If you get someone to read the questions to you, it becomes a "Jeopardy" kind of thing.

Another drawback to the old print-and-paper technology is found in the fact that you're forced to hold the thing all the time you're using it. If, for instance, you want a snack while using a book, you must put the book down in order to go get it. Putting the book down brings book activity to a dead stop until you pick up the book again. With television, of course, you can go right on watching and listening while you're making a sandwich.

But, if you stay with it, you might come to find charm in the quaintness of this bookish experience. Since this particular book is about television, some of the words will, through a kind of magic, convert themselves into remembered images. With patience and practice, reading this book will come to be a bit like channel surfing. Each question in the book might raise a visual memory of some half-forgotten moment spent in the company of that other higher technology—television.

Besides, not all advantages are on the side of television. With a book—once you've got the hang of it—you can control the pace of the experience. If you want to slow down, you can. If you want to speed up, you can. Some of the empowerment television viewers seek through the remote-control device is a standard feature of the book experience.

You can also think of this reading business as a return to older traditions, a visit to the world of your parents and grandparents, a bit like a return to the time when people made their own soap and candles.

So, return with us now to those days of yore. Grasp the book firmly, then proceed.

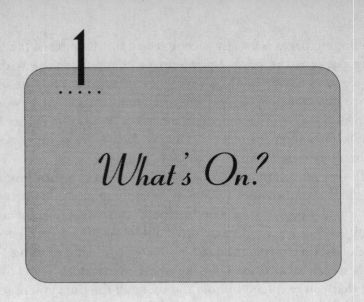

What's On?

"*I hate television. I hate it as much as peanuts.*
But I can't stop eating peanuts."

ORSON WELLES

This is a preliminary test, a warm-up exercise for what lies ahead in this book. If you know television, you should know the answers to at least seventy-five of the one hundred questions.

Regular viewers know television shows so well they can usually tell what's what, even from a brief synopsis. To get an idea of whether or not you qualify as a regular viewer, a couch potato, or a video addict, this little test offers some very brief plot sketches. From that, your job is to identify what show you would be watching, if you chose to watch the show described. So, read the following listings and supply the name of the show.

CHECKING CURRENT LISTINGS

1. Rowdy and Wishbone go for supplies. _____

2. "Bones," Mr. Sulu, and Chekov enter a timewarp. _____

3. Kramer, George, and Elaine plan a surprise for Jerry. _____

4. Jack, Janet, and Chrissy fool Mr. Furley. _____

5. Erica refuses Nick's long-awaited proposal. _____

6. Furillo and Joyce call off their engagement; Belker cleans up his
    act; Officer Bates has PMS. _____

7. Percy Dovetonsils gives a reading; the Nairobi Trio performs.
    Also featuring J. Walter Puppybreath. _____

8. New fall films previewed. Fashions sizzle. What's hot in music.
    Join John and Leeza for showbiz news.
    _____

9. Brandon and Brenda argue with Kelly and Steve over where to
    shop on Rodeo Drive. _____

10. Jethro and Elly May are worried when Duke gets worms.
    _____

11. Malloy and Reed report to Sgt. MacDonald for reassignment to
    South Central. _____

12. The Robinsons foil Dr. Zachary Smith's plans. _____

13. Kookie loses Bailey's and Spencer's cars. _____

14. Gomez punishes Pugsley for an act of kindness. _____

15. Ernie, Bert, and Grover learn about "9" from Mr. Hooper. _____

16. Sally and Buddy lose the script. Rob is in trouble for working overtime. _____

17. Moondoggie dents his board. _____

18. Mike Nelson gets waterlogged. _____

19. Bret and Bart split a pot. _____

20. Timmy's lost. His mom and dad, Ruth and Paul, set out to find him, with the help of you-know-who.

   _____

21. Louie assigns Banta to a bad cab. _____

22. Hoss takes violin lesson, drives brothers nuts. _____

23. Dr. White rapes Dr. Martin. Nurse Daniels shoots Dr. White. _____

24. Deborah Norville takes over cohost chair. _____

25. Kev gets even with Wayne; Josh gives a note to Gwendolyn. _____

26. Dr. Kiley and nurse Consuelo buy a birthday present for their boss. _____

27. Ed welcomes the Flying Wallendas, Marge and Gower Champion, and Kate Smith. _____

28. At last, Don Hollinger proposes to Ann Marie. _____

29. Segments include a Pat Paulsen campaign speech and "Take a Little Tea With Goldie." _____

30. Davy, Mickey, Mike, and Peter get zany, perform "Last Train to Clarksville." _____

31. David tries to bed Maddie, hilarity ensues. _____

32. Sgt. Saunders takes his platoon on a mission to rescue captured GIs. _____

33. Jaime Somers needs replacement parts. _____

34. Kimble extracts confession from one-armed man. _____

35. Lt. McMurphy is interviewed by Wayloo Marie Holmes. Guest star Nancy Sinatra sings "These Boots Are Made for Walkin'."

    _____

36. Principal Kaufman commends Dixon, his star history teacher; Alice Johnson learns valuable lesson about teaching. _____

37. Edward Asner appears as slave trader Captain Davies. _____

38. Chris and Mary Beth bicker—again. _____

39. Otis takes the pledge. Thelma Lou breaks a date. _____

40. Fish has indigestion; Wojo and Dietrich apprehend a werewolf; Levitt fails to measure up. _____

41. Fleischman and pilot O'Connell are stranded when she's forced to make an emergency landing. _____

42. Wood, Harlan, and Herman get naked. _____

43. Mr. Wilson is hopping mad—again. _____

44. Mr. Green Jeans brings a chicken. _____

45. Jim and Tammy Faye welcome Pat Boone. _____

46. David and Ricky go for malteds. _____

47. Rochester and Dennis plan a surprise for Mary. _____

48. Lou, Ted, and Murray plan a surpise for Mary. _____

49. Officer Foley plans a surprise for Mary. _____

50. Felix and Oscar have a date with the Pigeon sisters. _____

51. Toody and Muldoon escort foreign diplomat—with hilarious results. _____

52. Dick and Ed spring a trick on Erik Estrada. _____

53. 86 and 99 rescue Agent Larrabee. _____

54. Solo and Kuryakin trapped in abandoned warehouse. _____

55. Mr. Carlin insults Carol; Howard borrows a hanger.

_____

56. Richie, Potsie, and Ralph Malph apply for college admission.

_____

57. Tod and Buz take jobs picking fruit to pay for auto repairs.

_____

58. Scotty and Kelly blow their cover. _____

59. Tom Bradford gets writer's block; the kids help him with ideas.
   _____

60. Chuck and the gang of zanies (Jaye P. Morgan, Rex Reed, Jamie Farr) rate a nose whistler and two animal acts. _____

61. Sgt. Carter is in trouble with Colonel Gray, but our favorite private saves the day. _____

62. Les Nessman covers a Thanksgiving turkey drop.
   _____

63. Major Seth Adams sends Flint for help when the settlers are surrounded by hostile Indians. _____

64. McGarrett declares war on drug dealers. _____

65. Crockett and Tubbs declare war on drug dealers. _____

66. Former boxer takes a job as a domestic. _____

67. Don Diego sends Bernardo to trick Sgt. Garcia _____

68. Coach Ken Reeves argues with Principal Willis over the Carver High basketball budget. _____

69. Homer introduces a new drink at Moe's. _____

70. Segments feature the Mean Widdle Kid, Freddie the Freeloader, and Clem Kadiddlehopper. _____

71. Tim O'Hara fends off Lorelei's suspicions about Martin O'Hara's behavior. _____

72. Philbrick infiltrates a suspicious labor union. _____

73. Ethel plans a surprise for Fred—with a little help from her friend. _____

74. Detective's raincoat accidentally sent to the cleaners.

_____

75. The Log Lady makes another appearance. _____

76. Sheriff Hogg goes on a rampage. _____

77. Ensign Parker misunderstands an order. _____

78. Robin Colcord goes to jail; Rebecca freaks out. _____

79. Guests include Aunt Blabby, Michael Landon, Bob Hope. _____

80. James West and Artemus Gordon face nemesis, Dr. Loveless. _____

81. Complaints mount over Sgt. Yemana's coffee.

_____

82. The Boy Wonder is chilled by Dr. Freeze. _____

83. Jessica considers leaving Cabot Cove because of high crime rate. _____

84. McPike sends Terranova after Sonny Steelgrave.

_____

85. Pebbles and Bam-Bam adopt a dinosaur. _____

86. Theo and Cockroach succumb to peer pressure, but learn a valuable lesson. _____

87. Wally and Eddie succumb to peer pressure; Wally learns a lesson. _____

88. Gene and Roger review the career of Bruce Willis. _____

89. Diana's sister, Drusilla, is captured by Nazis. Major Steve Trevor called on to help. _____

90. Jimmy Olson holds the secret to saving Metropolis, but he's tied up. _____

91. Paul Lynde occupies center square. _____

92. Bentley Gregg leaves daughter Kelly in the care of Peter Tong, the butler; Howard Meachum comes calling. _____

93. The Kingfish has a spat with Sapphire. _____

94. Melmackian is captured. _____

95. Shredder has a plan to eliminate pizza. _____

96. Number 6 battles to preserve his individuality in "the village." _____

97. The Frug cooks lamb chops, chats. _____

98. Inspector Erskine and Agents Colby and Daniels infiltrate the mob. _____

99. Featuring the "Not Ready for Prime Time Players . . ." _____

100. Larry "Bud" Melman makes a brief appearance. _____

1. Rowdy and Wishbone go for supplies: **"Rawhide"**

2. "Bones," Mr. Sulu, and Chekov enter a time warp: **"Star Trek"**

3. Kramer, George, and Elaine plan a surprise for Jerry: **"Seinfeld"**

4. Jack, Janet, and Chrissy fool Mr. Furley: **"Three's Company"**

5. Erica refuses Nick's long-awaited proposal: **"All My Children"**

6. Furillo and Joyce call off their engagement; Belker cleans up his act; Officer Bates has PMS: **"Hill Street Blues"**

7. Percy Dovetonsils gives a reading; the Nairobi Trio performs. Also featuring J. Walter Puppybreath: **"The Ernie Kovacs Show"**

8. New fall films previewed. Fashions sizzle. What's hot in music. Join John and Leeza for showbiz news: **"Entertainment Tonight"**

9. Brandon and Brenda argue with Kelly and Steve over where to shop on Rodeo Drive: **"Beverly Hills, 90210"**

10. Jethro and Elly May are worried when Duke gets worms: **"The Beverly Hillbillies"**

11. Malloy and Reed report to Sgt. MacDonald for reassignment to South Central: **"Adam 12"**

12. The Robinsons foil Dr. Zachary Smith's plans: **"Lost in Space"**

13. Kookie loses Bailey's and Spencer's cars: **"77 Sunset Strip"**

14. Gomez punishes Pugsley for an act of kindness: **"The Addams Family"**

15. Ernie, Bert, and Grover learn about "9" from Mr. Hooper: **"Sesame Street"**

Answers

16. Sally and Buddy lose the script. Rob is in trouble for working overtime: **"The Dick Van Dyke Show"**

17. Moondoggie dents his board: **"Gidget"**

18. Mike Nelson gets waterlogged: **"Sea Hunt"**

19. Bret and Bart split a pot: **"Maverick"**

20. Timmy's lost. His mom and dad, Ruth and Paul, set out to find him, with the help of you-know-who: **"Lassie"**

21. Louie assigns Banta to a bad cab: **"Taxi"**

22. Hoss takes violin lesson, drives brothers nuts: **"Bonanza"**

23. Dr. White rapes Dr. Martin. Nurse Daniels shoots Dr. White: **"St. Elsewhere"**

24. Deborah Norville takes over cohost chair: **"The Today Show"**

25. Kev gets even with Wayne; Josh gives a note to Gwendolyn: **"The Wonder Years"**

26. Dr. Kiley and nurse Consuelo buy a birthday present for their boss: **"Marcus Welby"**

27. Ed welcomes the Flying Wallendas, Marge and Gower Champion, and Kate Smith: **"The Ed Sullivan Show"**

28. At last, Don Hollinger proposes to Ann Marie: **"That Girl"**

29. Segments include a Pat Paulsen campaign speech and "Take A Little Tea With Goldie": **"The Smothers Brothers Comedy Hour"**

30. Davy, Mickey, Mike, and Peter get zany, perform "Last Train to Clarksville": **"The Monkees"**

31. David tries to bed Maddie, hilarity ensues: **"Moonlighting"**

32. Sgt. Saunders takes his platoon on a mission to rescue captured GIs: **"Combat"**

33. Jaime Somers needs replacement parts: **"The Bionic Woman"**

34. Kimble extracts confession from one-armed man: **"The Fugitive"**

35. Lt. McMurphy is interviewed by Wayloo Marie Holmes. Guest star Nancy Sinatra sings "These Boots Are Made for Walkin'": **"China Beach"**

36. Principal Kaufman commends Dixon, his star history teacher; Alice Johnson learns a valuable lesson about teaching: **"Room 222"**

37. Edward Asner appears as slave trader Captain Davies: **"Roots"**

38. Chris and Mary Beth bicker—again: **"Cagney & Lacey"**

39. Otis takes the pledge. Thelma Lou breaks a date: **"The Andy Griffith Show"**

40. Fish has indigestion; Wojo and Dietrich apprehend a werewolf; Levitt fails to measure up: **"Barney Miller"**

41. Fleischman and pilot O'Connell are stranded when she's forced to make an emergency landing: **"Northern Exposure"**

42. Wood, Harlan, and Herman get naked: **"Evening Shade"**

Answers

43. Mr. Wilson is hopping mad—again: **"Dennis the Menace"**

44. Mr. Green Jeans brings a chicken: **"Captain Kangaroo"**

45. Jim and Tammy Faye welcome Pat Boone: **"PTL"**

46. David and Ricky go for malteds: **"The Adventures of Ozzie & Harriet"**

47. Rochester and Dennis plan a surprise for Mary: **"The Jack Benny Show"**

48. Lou, Ted, and Murray plan a surpise for Mary: **"The Mary Tyler Moore Show"**

49. Officer Foley plans a surprise for Mary: **"Mary Hartman, Mary Hartman"**

50. Felix and Oscar have a date with the Pigeon sisters: **"The Odd Couple"**

51. Toody and Muldoon escort foreign diplomat—with hilarious results: **"Car 54, Where Are You?"**

52. Dick and Ed spring a trick on Erik Estrada: **"TV's Bloopers and Practical Jokes"**

53. 86 and 99 rescue Agent Larrabee: **"Get Smart"**

54. Solo and Kuryakin trapped in abandoned warehouse: **"The Man from U.N.C.L.E."**

55. Mr. Carlin insults Carol; Howard borrows a hanger: **"The Bob Newhart Show"**

56. Richie, Potsie, and Ralph Malph apply for college admission: **"Happy Days"**

57. Tod and Buz take jobs picking fruit to pay for auto repairs: **"Route 66"**

58. Scotty and Kelly blow their cover: **"I Spy"**

59. Tom Bradford gets writer's block; the kids help him with ideas: **"Eight is Enough"**

60. Chuck and the gang of zanies (Jaye P. Morgan, Rex Reed, Jamie Farr) rate a nose whistler and two animal acts: **"The Gong Show"**

61. Sgt. Carter is in trouble with Colonel Gray, but our favorite private saves the day: **"Gomer Pyle, U.S.M.C."**

62. Les Nessman covers a Thanksgiving turkey drop: **"WKRP in Cincinnati"**

63. Major Seth Adams sends Flint for help when the settlers are surrounded by hostile Indians: **"Wagon Train"**

64. McGarrett declares war on drug dealers: **"Hawaii Five-0"**

65. Crockett and Tubbs declare war on drug dealers: **"Miami Vice"**

66. Former boxer takes job as a domestic: **"Who's the Boss?"**

67. Don Diego sends Bernardo to trick Sgt. Garcia: **"Zorro"**

68. Coach Ken Reeves argues with Principal Willis over the Carver High basketball budget: **"White Shadow"**

69. Homer introduces a new drink at Moe's: **"The Simpsons"**

70. Segments feature the Mean Widdle Kid, Freddie the Freeloader, and Clem Kadiddlehopper: **"The Red Skelton Show"**

71. Tim O'Hara fends off Lorelei's suspicions about Martin O'Hara's behavior: **"My Favorite Martian"**

72. Philbrick infiltrates a suspicious labor union: **"I Led Three Lives"**

73. Ethel plans a surprise for Fred—with a little help from her friend: **"I Love Lucy"**

74. Detective's raincoat accidentally sent to the cleaners: **"Columbo"**

75. The Log Lady makes another appearance: **"Twin Peaks"**

76. Sheriff Hogg goes on a rampage: **"The Dukes of Hazzard"**

77. Ensign Parker misunderstands an order: **"McHale's Navy"**

78. Robin Colcord goes to jail; Rebecca freaks out: **"Cheers"**

79. Guests include Aunt Blabby, Michael Landon, Bob Hope: **"The Tonight Show"**

80. James West and Artemus Gordon face nemesis, Dr. Loveless: **"The Wild, Wild West"**

81. Complaints mount over Sgt. Yemana's coffee: **"Barney Miller"**

82. The Boy Wonder is chilled by Dr. Freeze: **"Batman"**

83. Jessica considers leaving Cabot Cove because of high crime rate: **"Murder, She Wrote"**

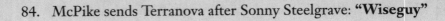
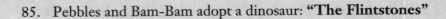

84. McPike sends Terranova after Sonny Steelgrave: **"Wiseguy"**

85. Pebbles and Bam-Bam adopt a dinosaur: **"The Flintstones"**

86. Theo and Cockroach succumb to peer pressure, but learn a valuable lesson: **"The Bill Cosby Show"**

87. Wally and Eddie succumb to peer pressure; Wally learns a lesson: **"Leave It to Beaver"**

88. Gene and Roger review the career of Bruce Willis: **"Siskel & Ebert At the Movies"**

89. Diana's sister, Drusilla, is captured by Nazis. Major Steve Trevor called on to help: **"Wonder Woman"**

90. Jimmy Olson holds the secret to saving Metropolis, but he's tied up: **"Superman"**

91. Paul Lynde occupies center square: **"Hollywood Squares"**

92. Bentley Gregg leaves daughter Kelly in the care of Peter Tong, the butler; Howard Meachum comes calling: **"Bachelor Father"**

93. The Kingfish has a spat with Sapphire: **"Amos 'n' Andy"**

94. Melmackian is captured: **"Alf"**

95. Shredder has a plan to eliminate pizza: **"Teenage Mutant Ninja Turtles"**

96. Number 6 battles to preserve his individuality in "the village": **"The Prisoner"**

97. The Frug cooks lamb chops, chats: **"The Frugal Gourmet"**

98. Inspector Erskine and Agents Colby and Daniels infiltrate the mob: **"The F.B.I."**

99. Featuring the "Not Ready for Prime Time Players": **"Saturday Night Live"**

100. Larry "Bud" Melman makes a brief appearance: **"Late Night With David Letterman"**

Scoring

75–100 Correct: Proceed with confidence.

50-74 Correct: Relax, the next test may prove easier.

25-49 Correct: You've apparently had other things to do besides watch TV.

0-24 Correct: You either haven't watched much TV, or you have a terrible memory.

Whatever your score, give the next chapter a try. It's fairly elementary, and it begins with the ABCs.

2

TV ABCs

"Television pollutes identity."
NORMAN MAILER

Down the years, around the clock, and through the alphabet, this is a grab bag test of all you know about television in its many times, guises, manifestations, and personalities. We'll start you off easy. If you're a channel surfer, you surely know your ABCs. Any viewer worth his salt ought to be able to get through the following alphabet of questions without too much trouble. If you know TV, then you'll probably know all twenty-six of the following, and the twenty-six following that, and so on. Can you make it from A to Z? From Z to A? This test will answer that question.

1. **Arnaz, Desi**
   What was his nationality? _____

2. **"Barnaby Jones"**
   Who played the title role? _____

3. **"Captain Kangaroo"**
   Who portrayed the Captain? _____

4. **"Death Valley Days"**
   Name two people who hosted it. _____ and
   _____

5. **"Eight Is Enough"**
   Who played the father? _____

6. **"Father Knows Best"**
   The kids' names were:_____ , _____ ,
   and _____

7. **"Gidget"**
   Who played her?_____

8. **"Hopalong Cassidy"**
   Can you name his horse?_____

9. **"I Dream of Jeannie"**
   One of its costars moved to "Dallas."
   Name him. _____

10. **"Jetsons, The"**
    Created by what animation team?_____

11. **"Kojak"**
    Kojak's most often repeated stock phrase._____

12. La Lanne, Jack
    He was among the first to do this kind of show.
    What kind of show? _____

13. "MacNeil-Lehrer Report, The"
    What network? _____

14. Nickelodeon
    A cable channel specializing in what kind of
    programming? _____

15. "Odd Couple, The"
    Who wrote the play on which it was based? _____

16. Parks, Bert
    When you hear his name, what song do you automatically
    think of? _____

17. "Queen for a Day" Name its host. _____

18. Rivera, Geraldo
    He often mentions his ethnic heritage, which is _____
    and _____

19. Soupy Sales
    His dogs were _____ and _____

20. "Twilight Zone"
    Its host was _____

21. "Undersea World of _____ , The"
    Fill in the blanks above.

22. "Vast Wasteland"
    It was a Federal Communications Commission chairman who
    uttered these words to describe television programming in the

early 1960s. Can you name him? _____

23. **"Waltons, The"**
The home of the Waltons was _____ Mountain.

24. **X**-Ray Vision
Superman had it. Who played him on TV?

_____

25. **"You Bet Your Life"**
What happened when contestants said the
secret word? _____

26. **ZZ** Top
Their career was resurrected and sustained by endless videos on
this cable channel. _____

If you did well on that journey through the alphabet, you're probably
eager to continue. Let's try again, this time working backward, from Z
to A.

27. **"Zorro"**
The Disney Zorro had a theme song that made the hit parade in
1958. The song went: "Zorro—the fox so cunning and
free/Zorro—make the sign of the _____ ."

28. **"Your Show of Shows"**
Name three of its four principal stars.

1. _____

2. _____

3. _____

29. **X** Brands
He was a character actor (you'd remember him if you saw his face) who played Pahoo-Ka-Ta-Wah, Indian sidekick to "Yancy _____" on this late-fifties series.

30. **"Welcome Back, Kotter"**
Who played Vinnie Barbarino? _____

31. **"Vinnie Barbarino"**
Barbarino, Horshack, Epstein, and "Boom-Boom" were collectively referred to as the " _____ ."

32. **"Uncle Buck"**
It only lasted through the '90-'91 season. It was adapted from the movie of the same name that starred _____ .

33. **"Twin Peaks"**
Her murder set the series in motion. _____

34. **"Sunday Morning"**
This CBS show has been on since 1984.
Its host is _____ .

35. **Rollins, Howard E. Jr.**
He plays Virgil Tibbs on "In the Heat of the Night."
His costar is _____ .

36. **"Quincy, M.E."**
Jack Klugman played him on this series that ran from 1976 through 1983. What does M.E. stand for?

_____

37. **"Profiles in Courage"**
This mid-sixties NBC series was based on a book written by an American president. Which president?

_____

38. **"Our Miss Brooks"**
    This show gave us our first look at an actor we were going to see a great deal of after that. He played Walter Denton.
    His name is _____ .

39. **"Now It Can Be Told"**
    Tabloid television/investigative reporting, hosted by _____ .

40. **"My Friend** _____ "
    The fifties gave us two shows whose titles began with the words "My Friend." Can you name them both?
    a. My Friend _____ "
    b. My Friend _____ "

41. **"Love Boat, The"**
    Fred Grandy played a character on this show before being elected to the U.S. Congress. What was the nickname of the character he played? _____

42. **"Kung Fu"**
    Master Po, played by Keye Luke, called his young pupil _____ .

43. **"Jeopardy!"**
    On "Jeopardy!" the first round is called Jeopardy, the second round is called _____ Jeopardy, and the third round is called _____ Jeopardy.

44. **"I Spy"**
    This was the first television series to star a black actor in a regular role. You know who he was, of course, but do you remember the occupation the two spies used as a cover for their espionage activities? _____

45. **"Hollywood Squares"**
    Who was the first regular host of this show? _____

46. "Golden Girls, The"
We might have guessed that the writers would locate a show about aging women in this American city.
Name it. _____

47. "Fresh Prince of _____ "
Fill in the blank above.

48. Edie Adams
She is the widow of TV innovator _____ .

49. "Dennis the Menace"
A two-part question: Who played Dennis on the TV show, and who created the comic strip on which the series was based?

_____   _____

50. "Cops"
Can you provide the name of the show's theme song?

_____

51. Brothers, Joyce
She was first seen, as a contestant, on these notorious quiz shows of the 1950s. Her category of expertise was boxing. Name the shows. _____ and _____

52. Arness, James
Before becoming Matt Dillon, he starred in a classic sci-fi film of the early 1950s. He played the title role.
Name the role and the film.

_____   _____

Feeling confident? Challenged? Then try A to Z, all over again.

53. **"Alice"**
Loosely based on the film *Alice Doesn't Live Here Anymore*.
a. Who played Alice in the film? _____
b. Who played Alice in the series? _____
c. (Extra credit) Who directed the film? _____

54. **BBC**
Where would PBS be without it? What do the initials BBC stand for? _____

55. **Cosell, Howard**
His most famous catchphrase was:
" _____. "

56. **Dinah Shore**
Her best-known sponsor was _____ .

57. **"Edge of Night, The"**
Which of the following actors *was not* a member of its cast?
a. Frank Gorshin;   b. Joanna Miles;   c. Lois Kibbee;
d. Forrest Tucker;   e. Forrest Compton _____

58. **Falwell, Jerry**
His nationally syndicated religious broadcast was called

_____ .

59. **Garagiola, Joe**
Before joining "The Today Show," he was a sportscaster and before that he was a baseball player. What position did he play?

_____

60. **"Helter Skelter"**
This was the top-rated presentation of the 1975–76 television season. It was a two-part adaption of a best-selling book. What was the show about? _____

61. **"Incredible Hulk, The"**
When David Banner (Bill Bixby) got angry he transformed himself into the Incredible Hulk, played by _____ .

62. **Jim Henson**
He created _____ .

63. **Kate Smith**
Back in the McCarthy era, she opened her prime-time show with
a patriotic song. What song? _____

64. **"Late Night With David Letterman"**
What's Larry Melman's nickname? _____

65. **Magnum, P.I.**
From 1981–1985, this giant of the silver screen played the voice
of Robin Masters, Magnum's employer.
Name that giant. _____

66. **"Newlywed Game, The"**
Who hosted this garbage? _____

67. **"On The Road With _____ _____ "**
He wrote a book with the same name. If you name the author,
you've filled in the blanks above.

68. **Perry Como**
a. His original occupation was _____ .
b. His theme song was _____ .

69. **"Quest, The"**
This short-lived western series starred a man who
was later to become Goldie Hawn's main squeeze.
He is _____ .

70. **Roy Rogers**

Surely you can name his theme song. _____

71. **S**ilverheels, Jay
He's most famous for his portrayal of _____,
sidekick to _____ .

72. **TBS**
Whose name is represented by the letter *T* in TBS?
_____
Who is his even more famous wife? _____

73. "**U**ntouchables, The"
This show prompted protests by an ethnic group.
Which ethnic group? _____

74. "**V**a-Va-Voom"
What TV character comes to mind when you hear
this phrase? _____

75. "**W**heel of Fortune"
Complete this phrase: "I want to buy a _____ . "

76. **X**avier Cugat
One of his protégés was the "coochy-coochy" girl,
better known as _____ .

77. "**Y**ou're in the Picture"
It was broadcast only once and was so bad that its host came on
the following week to apologize, saying, "Boy, did we bomb."
This was in 1961. Can you name the host?
_____

78. "**Z**ip a Dee Doo Dah"
It was the theme for a much-loved Disney production, repeated
often on "The Wonderful World of Disney." Name the title and
the main animated character. _____

And now, working backward, we'll work our way to A, and to the end of this test.

79. **Ziggy Stardust**
    In one of his many manifestations, this rock star made a host of videos that appeared on MTV. What name is he more commonly known by? _____

80. **Young, Alan**
    But what did Mr. Ed call him? _____

81. **X**, Malcolm
    The man who wrote *Roots* also did the definitive biography of Malcolm X. Who was that writer? _____

82. **"Wall Street Week"**
    Begun on PBS in 1972, this show recently celebrated its twentieth anniversary. Name the host. _____

83. **Vanna** _____
    Vanna who? Is there any other?

84. **UHF**
    What do the initials stand for? _____

85. **"Toast of the Town"**
    This was the original name of a Sunday night staple better known as _____ .

86. **"Sea Hunt"**
    We were to see quite a bit of him in years to come, but this was his first TV hit. Who is he? _____

87. **"Rich Man, Poor Man—Book I"**
Based on the Irwin Shaw novel, it was one of the biggest hits of the 1976 season.
The "rich" brother was played by _____ .
The "poor" brother was played by _____ .

88. **"Quantum Leap"**
When Dr. Sam Beckett took the "quantum leap," what did he leap through? _____

89. **"Peter Gunn"**
Who wrote the memorable and popular theme music?

_____

90. **"Omnibus"**
If it was TV and it was highbrow culture, then it was hosted by a Brit. This was very Highbrow Culture on fifties television. Name that Brit. _____

91. **"Night Court"**
"Bull" Shannon's real first name? _____

92. **MacGyver**
What was MacGyver's first name? _____

93. **Lawrence Welk**
Two favorites with Welk fans. Myron Florin played _____ .
Jo Ann Castle played _____ .

94. **"Kate and Allie"**
Both stars had success on television prior to this show. Susan St. James had a hit with _____ and Jane Curtin was well-known for her work on _____ .

95. "Jake and the Fatman"
Did you know that William Conrad (The Fatman) was once the radio voice of a western hero?
Which hero? _____

96. "In Living Color"
It is, in part, a family affair featuring Keenan Ivory, Damon, Kim, and S.W. What is their last name, and what's the network?

_____

97. "Hazel"
Hazel was played by a star of Broadway.
Can you name her? _____

98. Garry Moore
He launched the career of this much-loved comedienne.
Her name? _____

99. "Famous Adventures of Mr. Magoo, The"
Who was the voice of Magoo? _____

100. "Entertainment Tonight"
The male host is _____ .
The female host is _____ .

101. "Dudley Do-Right"
This cartoon character got his start on another Jay Ward creation. Name that show. _____
(Extra credit: Can you name Dudley's horse?_____)

102. "Casper, the Friendly Ghost"
Costarring his friend _____ , the Good Little Witch.

103. **B**oothe, Powers
He played a cult leader in a CBS miniseries entitled "The Guyana Tragedy."
What cult leader was that? _____

104. **A**rquette, Cliff
The character he created hailed from Mt. Idy, Ohio. Each week he read a letter from Mama. He was a regular on "The Jack Paar Show," and on "Hollywood Squares." What was the name of the character that made him famous?_____

Answers

1. Desi Arnaz was **Cuban**.

2. **Buddy Ebsen** played the title role in "Barnaby Jones."

3. **Bob Keeshan** played the much beloved Captain Kangaroo.

4. If you named any two of the four hosts of "Death Valley Days," you get credit for the right answer. They were: **Stanley Andrews** (as the "Old Ranger"), **Ronald Reagan**, **Robert Taylor**, and **Dale Robertson**.

5. **Dick Van Patten** played the father in "Eight Is Enough."

6. The kids' names in this all-American fifties series were **Betty**, **Jim, Jr.**, and **Kathy**. Extra credit if you knew their nicknames: **Princess**, **Bud**, and **Kitten**. (You probably didn't know Jim, Jr. as Jim, Jr. I didn't either. Always thought of him as Bud.)

7. The TV Gidget was **Sally Field**.

8. Hoppy's white horse was named **Topper**.

9. The "I Dream of Jeannie" costar who later starred in "Dallas" was Mary Martin's son, **Larry Hagman**.

10. "The Jetsons" was created and produced by **William Hanna** and **Joseph Barbera**.

11. Though one of his trademarks was sucking on a lollipop, another thing Kojak often did was say, **"Who loves ya, baby."**

12. Jack La Lanne was among the first to do an **exercise/physical fitness** show.

13. "The MacNeil-Lehrer Report" is on **PBS**.

14. Nickelodeon is a cable channel specializing in **children's programming and reruns.**

15. "The Odd Couple" was based on a highly successful play by **Neil Simon.**

16. Once the host of "Balance Your Budget," Bert Parks is best remembered for his starring role in the "Miss America Pageant", featuring the theme song, **"Here She Comes."**

17. **Jack Bailey** was the host of the sentimental "Queen for a Day."

18. Geraldo Rivera is **Jewish** and **Puerto Rican**.

19. Soupy Sales's canine puppet pets were **White Fang and Black Tooth.**

20. The original "Twilight Zone" was hosted by **Rod Serling**.

21. "The Undersea World of **Jacques Cousteau**" was an Emmy winner in the 1971–72 season.

22. FCC chairman **Newton Minow** used the words "Vast Wasteland" to describe television programmming in the early 1960s.

23. The home of the large Walton family was **Walton's** Mountain. The show grew out of the success of a 1971 Christmas special, "The Homecoming," by Earl Hamner, Jr.

24. **George Reeves** played the TV Superman with X-ray vision.

25. When contestants on "You Bet Your Life" said the secret word **a duck came down and they won $50.**

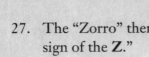

Answers

26. The career of ZZ Top was reinvigorated by **MTV**.

27. The "Zorro" theme song exhorted this foxlike hero to "make the sign of the **Z**."

28. The four main stars of "Your Show of Shows" were **Sid Caesar, Imogene Coca, Carl Reiner, and Howard Morris**.

29. X Brands played the Indian sidekick in "Yancy **Derringer**."

30. Vinnie Barbarino was played by **John Travolta,** who went on to movie stardom in *Saturday Night Fever*.

31. Chronic underachievers, Vinnie and pals were referred to as the **"sweathogs."**

32. *Uncle Buck*, the movie, starred **John Candy**.

33. **Laura Palmer** was the name of the teenager whose murder formed the plotline of this 1990 prime-time serial.

34. The host of "Sunday Morning" is **Charles Kuralt**.

35. **Carroll O'Connor** costars with Howard E. Rollins, Jr. in this TV crime drama based on a 1967 movie of the same name.

36. M.E. stands for **medical examiner**, a profession most often associated with a coroner's office.

37. *Profiles in Courage* was written by **John F. Kennedy**.

38. Moving from the radio version to TV in 1952, **Richard Crenna** played Madison High student Walter Denton.

39. "Now It Can Be Told" was hosted by **Geraldo Rivera**.

40. "My Friend **Irma**" debuted in 1952 and "My Friend **Flicka**" was first seen in 1956.

41. Also known as yeoman purser Smith, Fred Grandy's nickname in "The Love Boat" was "**Gopher**."

42. Master Po called his young pupil **Grasshopper**.

43. The second round on this popular syndicated game show developed by Merv Griffin is called **Double** Jeopardy; the third and last round is **Final** Jeopardy.

44. Bill Cosby played Alexander Scott, who was a **tennis trainer** for **tennis pro**, Kelly Robinson, played by Robert Culp.

45. The first regular host of this TV version of tick-tack-toe was **Peter Marshall**.

46. "The Golden Girls," a pioneering show in which all the lead characters were women over fifty, was set in **Miami**.

47. Rap musician, Will Smith stars in this sitcom called "Fresh Prince of **Bel Air**."

48. Edie Adams is the widow of **Ernie Kovacs**.

49. **Jay North** played the young, mischievous Dennis Mitchell in this series based on the comic strip by **Hank Ketcham**.

50. The theme song of "Cops" is "**Bad Boys**."

51. Dr. Joyce Brothers was first seen on TV as a contestant on "**The $64,000 Question**" and "**The $64,000 Challenge**."

52. Before settling into his long-lived character in "Gunsmoke," James Arness played the title role in *The Thing*.

53. **Ellen Burstyn** played Alice in the film and **Linda Lavin** played Alice in the TV series. Extra credit for naming **Martin Scorsese** as the director of the 1974 film.

54. BBC stands for the **British Broadcasting Corporation**.

55. Howard Cosell's most famous catchphrase was: **"Tell it like it is."**

56. Dinah Shore's best-known sponsor was **Chevrolet**.

57. **(d) Forrest Tucker** was not a member of "The Edge of Night" cast.

58. In the early days, evangelist Jerry Falwell's syndicated religious program was called **"The Old-Time Gospel Hour."**

59. Joe Garagiola was a second-string **catcher** for the St. Louis Cardinals before he became a broadcaster.

60. "Helter Skelter" was the story of the **Tate/LaBianca murders**.

61. The Incredible Hulk was played by a former Mr. America, **Lou Ferrigno**.

62. Kermit and Miss Piggy were just two of **The Muppets** created by Jim Henson.

63. Kate Smith opened her prime-time show, **"The Kate Smith Evening Hour,"** with a stirring rendition of "God Bless America." Extra credit if you can name the song that opened her daytime show: **"When the Moon Comes Over the Mountain."**

64. Larry Melman's nickname is **"Bud."**

65. The film giant who was the voice of Robin Masters was **Orson Welles**.

66. The tasteless but long-running "Newlywed Game" was hosted by **Bob Eubanks**.

67. The host of "Sunday Morning" (see question #34) has also taken us "On the Road With **Charles Kuralt**." Mr. Kuralt also wrote the book.

68. Perry Como began as a **barber**; when he hosted his popular 1950s musical/variety show his theme song was **"Dream Along With Me."**

69. **Kurt Russell** played one of two brothers separated while still young in "The Quest," created by Tracy Keenan Wynn.

70. Roy Rogers's theme song was **"Happy Trails to You."**

71. Jay Silverheels is most famous for his role as **Tonto**, sidekick to **the Lone Ranger**.

72. The letter *T* in TBS stands for **(Ted) Turner,** who is married to **Jane Fonda**.

73. "The Untouchables" offended **Italian-Americans**.

74. "Va-Va-Voom" was a favorite saying of **Ed Norton**, played by Art Carney in "The Honeymooners."

75. A phrase often heard on "Wheel of Fortune" is: "I want to buy a **vowel**."

76. Xavier Cugat's "coochy-coochy" girl was **Charo**.

77. **Jackie Gleason** was the embarrassed host of "You're in the Picture."

78. "Zip a Dee Doo Dah" was the theme for *Song of the South*, the main animated character of which was **Br'er Rabbit**.

79. Ziggy Stardust is also known as **David Bowie**.

80. Mr. Ed called actor Alan Young, **Wilbur**.

81. **Alex Haley** wrote *Roots* and *The Autobiography of Malcolm X*.

82. The host and moderator of "Wall Street Week" is **Louis Rukeyser**.

83. America's favorite letter turner is Vanna **White**.

84. UHF stands for **ultrahigh frequency**.

85. Officially titled "The Toast of the Town" until 1955, **"The Ed Sullivan Show"** was the longest-running variety show in TV history—from June 1948 through June 1971.

86. The father of Beau and Jeff, the star of "Sea Hunt" was **Lloyd Bridges**.

87. In "Rich Man, Poor Man—Book I," the rich brother, Rudy Jordache, was played by **Peter Strauss** and the poor brother, Tom Jordache, was played by **Nick Nolte**.

88. In "Quantum Leap," Dr. Beckett leapt through **time**.

89. **Henry Mancini** wrote the theme music for "Peter Gunn."

90. The British host of "Omnibus" was **Alistair Cooke**.

91. Court officer "Bull" Shannon's real first name was **Nostradamus**, and he was played by actor Richard Moll.

92. Richard Dean Anderson played **Angus** MacGyver. The series was created by Henry Winkler (of "Happy Days" fame) and John Rich.

93. Lawrence Welk fans will remember that Myron Floren played the **accordion** and Jo Ann Castle played **ragtime piano**.

94. "Kate and Allie" star Susan St. James had a hit with **"McMillan and Wife."** Jane Curtin was well-known for her work on **"Saturday Night Live."**

95. William Conrad was once the radio voice of **Matt Dillon**.

96. The offbeat comedy series "In Living Color" was created by and features Keenan Ivory **Wayans**, along with his brother, Damon **Wayans**, his sister, Kim **Wayans**, and his brother Shawn (S.W.) **Wayans**. It is shown on the Fox network.

97. Hazel was played by **Shirley Booth**.

98. Garry Moore launched the career of **Carol Burnett**.

99. **Jim Backus** was the voice of Mr. Magoo.

100. The male host of "Entertainment Tonight" is **John Tesh**. The female host is **Leeza Gibbons**.

101. Dudley Do-Right was first seen on **"Bullwinkle."** Dudley's horse was named **Horse**.

102. Casper, the Friendly Ghost, shared many adventures with his friend **Wendy**, the Good Little Witch.

103. The cult leader played by Powers Boothe was **Jim Jones**.

104. **Charley Weaver** was the character Cliff Arquette created that made him famous.

Perhaps that wasn't so easy. Many things were familiar, but some things were a bit obscure. If you got more than half of them right, you were doing pretty well.

Scoring

75–104 Correct: Now we know our ABCs, pretty much.

40–74 Correct: Either too young to know your letters, or too old to remember.

0–39 Correct: As an authority on TV trivia, you're still in "Romper Room."

Tater Tots

*"Won't you be, won't you be, please won't you be
my neighbor."*
"The Neighbor Song," by Fred Rogers

*"No one under eighteen will be murdered
on this show."*
Disclaimer issued by producers of
"Freddy's Nightmares"

You might as well admit it—you spent a good chunk of your child-hood watching television. In fact, according to most recent research, you spent about twenty-four hours a week in front of the tube, and that's a conservative estimate. One out of seven days during your "wonder years" were spent in front of the tube. By the time you graduated from high school, you'd witnessed nearly half a million acts of violence. You were sold a lot of sugar-saturated cereal and various lines of toys, from action-adventure heroes you'd seen on Saturday morning to video games that let you be part of your TV set. Did any of that stay with you? Questions in this chapter—and the answers you pro-vide—will give a clue as to how much you watched, and how much you remember.

The problem with constructing tests for this chapter is that we weren't all kids at the same time. Nearly four generations of children have passed through TV Land so far. What one generation remembers and treasures is forgotten by the next. You have to be of a certain age to remember Winky Dink. Younger people will fondly recall the Scooby Doos, but that name will mean nothing to many of their elders.

So you're going to miss questions in this test, no matter what age you are.

But you're also going to know more than you think you know, even if you haven't watched kid-vid since you were a tot. You're going to know some of this stuff through your kids, if you're a parent. You're going to know some of these cartoon characters through advertising, or through marketing in the stores around the holidays. That birthday present for your niece or nephew? Chances are it was a toy developed in conjunction with some Saturday morning show—GI Joes, Hot Wheels, Smurfs, Littles, Pound Puppies, Cabbage Patch Kids, Rainbow Brite. If you would know what it is to be a kid in America in the second half of the twentieth century, you must visit TV Land. This test begins that exploration. We'll begin with generics.

Test Number 1: **WHAT IS THAT THING?**

Boy, kids, do you remember when we all believed everything we saw on TV? We believed in all kinds of creatures, even when we weren't quite sure what they were. We believed that all kinds of animals could talk. Remember? Well, we'll see if you remember the characters listed on the left and if you can match them up to the correct things on the right. (You're not expected to get them all; some were before your time, and some were after.)

1. Winnie the Pooh _____   a. monkey

2. Heckle and Jeckle _____   b. clown

3. Eeyore _____   c. dragon

4. McBaker _____   d. frog

5. Orbots _____   e. mouse

6. Curious George _____   f. cat

7. Dumbo _____   g. dog

8. Magilla _____   h. humanoid/robot

9. The Littles _____   i. bird (any species)

10. Lancelot Link _____   j. bear

11. Hoppity Hooper _____   k. fish (any species)

12. Kermit _____   l. dinosaur

13. Clarabell _____   m. monster

14. Snagglepuss _____   n. bunny

15. Quick Draw McGraw _____   o. elephant

16. Kissyfur _____   p. ape or gorilla

17. Astro _____   q. witch

18. Jabberjaw _____   r. horse

19. Hong Kong Phooey _____   s. raisins

20. Marmaduke _____   t. lion

21. Sabrina _____   u. rat

22. Gentle Ben _____   v. chipmunk

23. Garfield _____   w. donkey

24. Sylvester _____   x. dolphin

25. Odie _____

26. Fury _____

27. Frankenstein Jr. _____

28. Mr. Cool _____

29. Foofur _____

30. Dino _____

31. Flipper _____

32. Broom Hilda _____

33. Dirk the Daring _____

34. Ollie (of Kukla, Fran, and Ollie) _____

35. Dink _____

36. Chip and Dale _____

37. White Fang and Black Tooth _____

38. Speedy Gonzales _____

39. Woodstock _____

40. Leader-1 _____

41. Tobor _____

42. Mighty Manfred _____

43. Stretch, Beebop, A.C., and Red _____

44. Bozo _____

45. The Biskitts _____

46. Tearalong _____

47. Alvin, Simon, and Theodore _____

48. Scooby Doov

49. Splinter _____

50. Spike & Tike, Droopy and Drippy _____

51. Goofy _____

52. Transformers _____

53. Wildfire _____

54. Voltron _____

55. Boo Boo _____

56. Yukk _____

57. Conky _____

58. Flicka _____

59. Thumper _____

60. Pluto _____

Test Number 2: BUDDIES, PALS, BEST OF FRIENDS

Okay, boys and girls. Now we'll try something else. We're going to have a little test of friendship. Friends are good. Friends are nice. We can count on friends to come through in a pinch. Can I count on you to match up the kid-show pals in the little test below? Just remember, there's no harm in not getting them all. We all learn from our mistakes.

1. Jonny Quest _____
2. Cecil _____
3. Captain Kangaroo _____
4. Mr. Rogers _____
5. Pee Wee _____
6. Fred Flintstone _____
7. Crusader Rabbit _____
8. Hopalong Cassidy _____
9. The Green Hornet _____

a. Terry the Terradactyl
b. Mr. Baxter and Debby
c. Rags the Tiger
d. Henry Bigg
e. Bullwinkle
f. Marty
g. Buddy
h. Megaman
i. Brittany, Eleanor, Jeanette

10. Ernest P. Worrell _____   j. Ikky Mudd

11. Kevin/Captain N _____   k. Gabby Hayes

12. Captain Midnight _____   l. Mr. McFeely

13. Tom Terrific _____   m. Mr. Greenjeans

14. Bert _____   n. Ernie

15. Spin _____   o. Beany

16. Rocky _____   p. Vern

17. The Littles _____   q. Kato

18. Little Rosey _____   r. Hadji

19. Beaver Cleaver _____   s. Whitey

20. Alvin, Simon, Theodore _____   t. Barney Rubble

Test Number 3: FOES AND ARCHENEMIES

Here's a fun one, boys and girls. Match the characters or forces pitted against one another.

1. Smurfs _____   a. The Joker

2. Dudley Do-Right _____   b. Grumplins of Grumplor

3. Care Bears _____   c. Gargamel

4. Teenage Mutant
   Ninja Turtles _____   d. Whoo Doo

5. Mickey Mouse _____   e. Silas Mayhem

6. The Road Runner _____   f. Snidely Whiplash

7. Bugs Bunny _____   g. Black Bart

8. Monchichis _____   h. Wile E. Coyote

9. Weenie the Genie
   (of "Lidsville") _____   i. Dark Heart

10. Jamie Jaren
    ("Lazer Tag Academy") _____   j. Lex Luthor

11. Jason of Star Command _____   k. Elmer Fudd

12. Jayce and the
    Wheeled Warriors _____   l. Boris and Natasha

13. Kevin/Captain N _____   m. Sylvester

14. Batman _____   n. Tom

15. Superman _____   o. Shredder

16. The Lone Ranger _____   p. Dr. Dread

17. Rocky and Bullwinkle _____   q. Dragos

18. Tweety _____   r. Monster Minds

19. Jerry _____   s. Motherbrain

20. The Drak Pack _____   t. The Cavendish Gang

Do you know how to say "miscellany"? Do you know what it means? If not, then you might be a little mixed up. But don't worry, you'll get the hang of it. If you get discouraged, just try a little harder. If you miss several in a row, you were probably out playing, studying, tidying up your room, or practicing the piano when those shows were on.

1. Complete the following. "George, George, George of the Jungle, Watch out for that _____ ."

2. He and the show were known as "Linus the _____ ."

3. Punky Brewster's pal was named _____ .

4. Casper, the _____ ;
   Wendy, the _____ ;
   and Nightmare, the _____ .

5. This was Ed Norton's favorite TV show. Complete the title. "Captain Video and His _____ ."

6. Lancelot Link was aided by a rock band called_____ .

7. Name Garfield's "owner." _____

8. Where do the Gummi Bears live? _____

9. What's the name of Gumby's horse? _____

10. What was the name of George of the Jungle's elephant? _____

11. Where do the Care Bears live? _____

12. Who played Captain Kangaroo all those years? _____

13. Who sponsored Captain Midnight? _____

14. "Camp Candy" has a head camp counselor. That animated character's voice is provided by what actor? _____

15. The Archies were responsible for what hit record?

    _____

16. Who are these guys? Donnie Wahlberg, Jordan Knight, Jonathan Knight, Joe McIntrye, and Dannie Wood. _____

17. Who are these guys? Mickey Dolenz, Mike Nesmith, Peter Tork, and Davy Jones. _____

18. The guy who played Mr. Peepers was also the guy who provided the voice of "Underdog." If you know one, you know the other. Do you know one? _____

19. His was the most famous and ubiquitous voice in animation. He played Sylvester, Bugs Bunny, and Barney Rubble, among many others. Who was he? _____

20. They are the most prolific producers of television cartoons, and they were the first to win an Emmy for doing so. I'll give you half the team; you provide the other half. Hanna/ _____

21. Snagglepuss was a regular on "Quick Draw McGraw," and his most oft repeated expression was "Heavenths to _____ !"

22. On what show do you find the Snuffleupagus? _____

23. The Stooges: Larry, Moe, Curley, and later _____

24. Of the following, which *is not* a Disney production: a. *Snow White*; b. *Song of the South*; c. *101 Dalmations*; d. *Fievel: An American Tale*. _____

25. Hoppity Hooper's sidekicks were a bear named _____ and a fox named _____ .

26. Hopalong Cassidy's horse was named _____ .

27. Back in the sixties, it was "The _____ Ant/ _____ Squirrel Show."

28. Not only were there two movies, but there was also a cartoon show called "The Attack of the Killer Tomatoes." In the cartoon, the villain's name is _____ .

29. "Wheelie and the Chopper Bunch" was a mid-seventies show. Who or what was "Wheelie"? _____

30. What do the Teenage Mutant Ninja Turtles eat? _____

31. Iota transformed himself into _____ to fight evil.

32. It was another Hanna/Barbera offering about an all-girl rock group known as "Josie and the _____ ."

33. Who was the creator of the Muppets?_____

34. George, Jane, Judy, and Elroy were_____ .

35. In the "Charlie Brown" shows and specials, what is Lucy's last name?_____

36. On "The Partridge Family," which kid was the redhead?_____

37. On what show would you have encountered characters named "Chairy" and "Globey"?_____

38. This Disney character left the mark of the Z. Who is he?

_____

39. This childhood hero was known by a silver bullet. Who is he?_____

40. What are blue, live in the forest, and are pursued by the mean and nasty Scruple?_____

41. On what show would you have found Jem/Jerica, the Holograms, the Misfits, and Pizzazz?_____

42. "The Super Mario Brothers Super Show" was part animation, part live action. In the live-action segments, a well-known professional wrestler (and friend of Cyndi Lauper) played Mario. Do you know his name?_____

43. Lois Lane, Perry White, and Jimmy Olsen all worked at_____.

44. It was this stuff, not Lois Lane, that made Superman weak in the knees. What stuff?_____

45. Which of the following *is not* a toy company/kid show advertiser: a. Coleco   b. Kenner   c. Glaxo   d. Galoob   e. Mattel _____

46. He starred as the Lone Ranger on television._____

47. He starred as Superman on '50s television._____

48. He starred as Batman on '60s television._____

49. Snoopy, Lucy, Peppermint Patty, Charlie Brown, Woodstock, and Linus are all_____.

50. Gobots from Gobotron are manufactured by _____.

51. Complete the following: "I don't wanna grow up. I'm a _____ kid."

52. What show would you have been watching if you encountered Mr. Peebles and Ogee?_____ .

53. Rebo the Clown and magician Mark Wilson could be found in "The Magic Land of _____ ."

54. Give or take five years, when did "The Flintstones" first appear on television?_____

55. Fred and Wilma had a child named_____ , and Barney and Betty had a child named _____ .

56. The Rattler, the Owl and the Pussycat, Number One, and Jack-in-the-Box were all villains fought by _____ .

57. What was the name of the dance created by Soupy Sales?
_____

58. Tinker, Debbie, and Mark all rode in the flying car known as
_____ .

59. Complete the following: "When you wish upon a star, makes
_____ .
When you wish upon a star, your
_____ ."

60. How did Spiderman get his super powers? _____

61. "Romper Room" was presided over by Miss_____ .

Test Number 5:
WHAT DO THE FOLLOWING HAVE IN COMMON?

1. Miguel Ratoncito, Mikkel Mus, Kiki Kuchi, Michael Maus, and Topolino are all _____ .

2. "Huckleberry Hound," "Quick Draw McGraw," "Yogi Bear," "The Flintstones," and "The Jetsons" are all cartoon shows produced by_____.

3. Superman, Batman and Robin, Aquaman, Wonder Woman, Marvin and Wendy, and Wonder Dog were all part of

   _____.

4. Zan and Jayna, Gleek, and the Wondertwins were all part of

   _____.

5. Sharon, Bobby, Lonny, Annette, Darlene, Cubby, Karen, and Don were all_____.

6. Jiminy Cricket, Geppetto, and Monstro were all characters in

   _____.

7. Ernie, Bert, Grover, and Oscar can all be found on

   _____.

8. Weird Harold, Mush Mouth, and Donald were all characters on_____.

9. Morticia, Gomez, Pugsley, Wednesday, and Uncle Fester were all members of_____.

10. Herman, Lily, Eddie, and Marilyn were all_____.

Test Number 6: **SIMPSON MANIA**

Some people won't let their children watch "The Simpsons," and it's perhaps more for adults than it is for kids, but if you like the show, you'll know most of the answers to this little quiz.

1. A cartoon within a cartoon. Name Bart Simpson's favorite cartoon show. _____

2. Name the bootlicking assistant to Mr. Burns, Homer's boss._____

3. Where Homer does his drinking. _____

4. The actress who performs the voice of Marge Simpson. _____

5. The name of the Simpson family dog. _____

6. The brand of beer Homer drinks. _____

7. Bart's teacher's name. _____

8. The instrument Lisa plays._____

9. The Simpsons' next-door neighbors._____

10. The creator of "The Simpsons," cartoonist _____ .

Test Number 7:
ONCE UPON A TIME, IN A LAND FAR, FAR AWAY . . .

While you were watching all that television (and, no doubt, sitting too near the screen), did you notice where your favorite characters lived? The next short quiz will give you some idea.

1. The Flintstones live in the prehistoric city of _____ .

2. Superman (and Clark Kent) live in the city of_____ .

3. Batman (and Bruce Wayne) live in the city of _____ .

4. The Simpsons live in the city of_____ .

5. The Jetsons live in the _____ Apartments.

6. Howdy Doody's hometown. _____

7. Kukla, Ollie, Fletcher Rabbit, Beulah the Witch, and Madame Ooglepuss were all _____ .

8. Sky King and Penny lived at the _____ Ranch.

9. Where do Archie, Jughead, Veronica, Betty, and Reggie go to school?_____

10. ALF contrasted American culture with that of his home planet. What was his home planet?_____

Test Number 8: **DISNEY IMPRESSIONS**

You weren't a kid in America if you didn't grow up with Walt Disney, surely the greatest purveyor of children's entertainment in the history of the world. This next short test will take a spot-reading of how much of that stuff stayed with you.

1. He was the duck professor who introduced many of Disney's more educational features. _____

2. He's the head of the Disney Corporation._____

3. The Four Lands at Disneyland are _____ , _____ , _____ , and _____ .

4. Who played Davy Crockett in the fifties?_____

5. Who played Davy Crockett in the eighties?_____

6. Now in video stores everywhere, these two features were back-to-back hits for Disney animators in 1991 and 1992.
   Name them._____ and _____

7. Who sang the title song in *Beauty and the Beast*?_____

8. Who did the voice of the genie in *Aladdin*?_____

9. Who are Donald Duck's nephews? _____

10. The original "Absent-Minded Professor" was played by
    _____ and _____ played the character in the made-for-television sequel.

Say, kids, wasn't that fun? Now it's time to check your answers. Just remember, it doesn't really matter how well you did, so long as you did your best. Until next time . . .

Answers

Test Number 1: **WHAT IS THAT THING?**

1. Winnie the Pooh: **(j) bear**

2. Heckle and Jeckle: **(i) bird**

3. Eeyore: **(w) donkey**

4. McBaker: **(g) dog**

5. Orbots: **(h) humanoid/robot**

6. Curious George: **(a) monkey**

7. Dumbo: **(o) elephant**

8. Magilla: **(p) gorilla**

9. The Littles: **(h) humaniod/robot**

10. Lancelot Link: **(a) monkey**

11. Hoppity Hooper: **(d) frog**

12. Kermit: **(d) frog**

13. Clarabell: **(b) clown**

14. Snagglepuss: **(t) lion**

15. Quick Draw McGraw: **(r) horse**

16. Kissyfur: **(j) bear**

17. Astro: **(g) dog**

18. Jabberjaw: **(k) fish**

19. Hong Kong Phooey: **(g) dog**

20. Marmaduke: **(g) dog**

21. Sabrina: **(q) witch**

22. Gentle Ben: **(j) bear**

23. Garfield: **(f) cat**

24. Sylvester: **(f) cat**

25. Odie: **(g) dog**

26. Fury: **(r) horse**

27. Frankenstein Jr.: **(h) humanoid/robot**

28. Mr. Cool: **(g) dog**

29. Foofur: **(g) dog**

30. Dino: **(l) dinosaur**

31. Flipper: **(x) dolphin**

32. Broom Hilda: **(q) witch**

33. Dirk the Daring: **(r) horse**

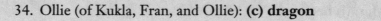
34. Ollie (of Kukla, Fran, and Ollie): **(c) dragon**

35. Dink: **(l) dinosaur**

36. Chip and Dale: **(v) chipmunk**

37. White Fang and Black Tooth: **(g) dog**

38. Speedy Gonzales: **(e) mouse**

39. Woodstock: **(i) bird**

40. Leader-1: **(h) humanoid/robot**

41. Tobor: **(h) humanoid/robot**

42. Mighty Manfred: **(g) dog**

43. Stretch, Beebop, A.C., and Red: **(s) raisins**

44. Bozo: **(b) clown**

45. The Biskitts: **(g) dog**

46. Tearalong: **(t) lion**

47. Alvin, Simon, and Theodore: **(v) chipmunk**

48. Scooby Doo: **(g) dog**

49. Splinter: **(u) rat**

50. Spike & Tike, Droopy and Drippy: **(g) dog**

51. Goofy: **(g) dog**

52. Transformers: **(h) humanoid/robot**

53. Wildfire: **(r) horse**

54. Voltron: **(h) humanoid/robot**

55. Boo Boo: **(j) bear**

56. Yukk: **(g) dog**

57. Conky: **(h) humanoid/robot**

58. Flicka: **(r) horse**

59. Thumper: **(n) bunny**

60. Pluto: **(g) dog**

Answers

Test Number 2: **BUDDIES, PALS, BEST OF FRIENDS**

1. Jonny Quest: **(r) Hadji**

2. Cecil: **(o) Beany**

3. Captain Kangaroo: **(m) Mr. Greenjeans**

4. Mr. Rogers: **(l) Mr. McFeely**

5. Pee Wee: **(a) Terry the Terradactyl**

6. Fred Flintstone: **(t) Barney Rubble**

7. Crusader Rabbit: **(c) Rags the Tiger**

8. Hopalong Cassidy: **(k) Gabby Hayes**

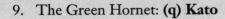

9. The Green Hornet: **(q) Kato**

10. Ernest P. Worrell: **(p) Vern**

11. Kevin/Captain N: **(h) Megaman**

12. Captain Midnight: **(j) Ikky Mudd**

13. Tom Terrific: **(b) Mr. Baxter and Debby**

14. Bert: **(n) Ernie**

15. Spin: **(f) Marty**

16. Rocky: **(e) Bullwinkle**

17. The Littles: **(d) Henry Bigg**

18. Little Rosey: **(g) Buddy**

19. Beaver Cleaver: **(s) Whitey**

20. Alvin, Simon, Theodore: **(i) Brittany, Eleanor, Jeanette**

Test Number 3: **FOES AND ARCHENEMIES**

1. Smurfs: **(c) Gargamel**

2. Dudley Do-Right: **(f) Snidely Whiplash**

3. Care Bears: **(i) Dark Heart**

4. Teenage Mutant Ninja Turtles: **(o) Shredder**

5. Mickey Mouse: **(g) Black Bart**

6. The Road Runner: **(h) Wile E. Coyote**

7. Bugs Bunny: **(k) Elmer Fudd**

8. Monchichis: **(b) Grumplins of Grumplor**

9. Weenie the Genie (of "Lidsville"): **(d) Whoo Doo**

10. Jamie Jaren ("Lazer Tag Academy"): **(e) Silas Mayhem**

11. Jason of Star Command: **(q) Dragos**

12. Jayce and the Wheeled Warriors: **(r) Monster Minds**

13. Kevin/Captain N: **(s) Motherbrain**

14. Batman: **(a) The Joker**

15. Superman: **(j) Lex Luthor**

16. The Lone Ranger: **(t) The Cavendish Gang**

17. Rocky and Bullwinkle: **(l) Boris and Natasha**

18. Tweety: **(m) Sylvester**

19. Jerry: **(n) Tom**

20. The Drak Pack: **(p) Dr. Dread**

Answers

1. "George, George, George of the Jungle, Watch out for that **tree**."

2. He and the show were known as "Linus the **Lionhearted**."

3. Punky Brewster's pal was named **Glomer**.

4. Casper, the **Friendly Ghost**; Wendy, the **Good Little Witch**; and Nightmare, the **Galloping Ghost**.

5. Ed Norton's favorite TV show was "Captain Video and His **Video Rangers**."

6. Lancelot Link was aided by a rock band called the **Evolution Revolution**.

7. Garfield's "owner": **John Arbuckle**.

8. The Gummi Bears live in **Dunwyn**.

9. The name of Gumby's horse is **Pokey**.

10. George of the Jungle's elephant was named **Shep**.

11. The Care Bears live in **Carealot**.

12. Captain Kangaroo was played by **Bob Keeshan**.

13. "Captain Midnight" was sponsored by **Ovaltine**.

14. "Camp Candy" has a head camp counselor whose voice is provided by **John Candy**.

15. The Archies were responsible for the hit record **"Sugar, Sugar."**

16. Donnie Wahlberg, Jordan Knight, Jonathan Knight, Joe McIntrye, and Dannie Wood are the **New Kids on the Block**.

17. Mickey Dolenz, Mike Nesmith, Peter Tork, and Davy Jones are **The Monkees**.

18. **Wally Cox** played Mr. Peepers and was the voice of "Underdog."

19. This famous voice belonged to **Mel Blanc**.

20. **Barbera** is the other half of this productive team.

21. Snagglepuss's favorite expression was "Heavenths to **Mergatroid**!"

22. The Snuffleupagus lives on **"Sesame Street."**

23. The Stooges: Larry, Moe, Curley, and later **Shemp**.

24. **(d)** *Fievel: An American Tale* is not a Disney production.

25. Hoppity Hooper's sidekicks were a bear named **Fillmore** and a fox named **Uncle Waldo**.

26. Hopalong Cassidy's horse was named **Topper**.

27. Back in the sixties, it was "The **Atom** Ant/**Secret** Squirrel Show."

28. **Dr. Putrid T. Gangreen** is the villain in the cartoon version of "The Attack of the Killer Tomatoes."

29. Wheelie was a **Volkswagen**.

30. The Teenage Mutant Ninja Turtles eat **pizza**.

31. Iota transformed himself into **Ultraman** to fight evil.

32. It was another Hanna/Barbera offering about an all-girl rock group known as "Josie and the **Pussycats**."

33. **Jim Henson** created the Muppets.

34. George, Jane, Judy, and Elroy were **"The Jetsons."**

35. Lucy's last name is **Van Pelt**.

36. **Danny** was the redheaded Partridge.

37. "Chairy" and "Globey" were regulars on **"Pee Wee's Playhouse."**

38. **Zorro** left the sign of the *Z*.

39. **The Lone Ranger** was known by a silver bullet.

40. **The Smurfs** were the blue forest creatures pursued by the mean and nasty Scruple.

41. You would have found Jem/Jerica, the Holograms, the Misfits, and Pizzazz on **"Jem."**

42. Cyndi Lauper's friend **Captain Lou Albano** played Mario.

43. Lois Lane, Perry White, and Jimmy Olsen all worked at the *Daily Planet*.

44. More powerful than Lois, **Kryptonite** made Superman weak in the knees.

45. **(c) Glaxo** is not a toy company/kid-show advertiser.

46. **Clayton Moore** was television's Lone Ranger.

47. On TV, Superman was played by **George Reeves**.

48. **Adam West** was TV's Batman.

49. Snoopy, Lucy, Peppermint Patty, Charlie Brown, Woodstock, and Linus are all **"Peanuts" characters**.

50. Gobots from Gobotron are manufactured by **Tonka Toys**.

51. "I don't wanna grow up. I'm a **Toys 'R' Us** kid."

52. Mr. Peebles and Ogee are on **"Magilla Gorilla."**

53. Rebo the Clown and magician Mark Wilson could be found in "The Magic Land of **Allakazam**."

54. "The Flintstones" first appeared on television in **1960**.

55. Fred and Wilma had a child named **Pebbles**, and Barney and Betty had a child named **Bamm Bamm**.

56. The Rattler, the Owl and the Pussycat, Number One, and Jack-in-the-Box were all villains fought by **Cool McCool**.

57. Soupy Sales created **The Soupy Shuffle**.

58. Tinker, Debbie, and Mark all rode in the flying car known as **Speed Buggy**.

59. "When you wish upon a star, makes **no difference who you are**. When you wish upon a star, your **dreams come true**."

60. Spiderman got his super powers when **he was bitten by a radioactive spider**.

61. In the fifties, Miss **Nancy** was the teacher on Romper Room. Later on, her daughter, Miss **Sally**, was the teacher seen by most children.

Test Number 5:
WHAT DO THE FOLLOWING HAVE IN COMMON?

Answers

1. Miguel Ratoncito, Mikkel Mus, Kiki Kuchi, Michael Maus, and Topolino are various foreign names for **Mickey Mouse**.

2. "Huckleberry Hound," "Quick Draw McGraw," "Yogi Bear," "The Flintstones," and "The Jetsons" are all cartoon shows produced by **Hanna-Barbera**.

3. Superman, Batman and Robin, Aquaman, Wonder Woman, Marvin and Wendy, and Wonder Dog were all part of **"The Justice League of America/Superfriends."**

4. Zan and Jayna, Gleek, and the Wondertwins were also all part of **"The Justice League of America/Superfriends."**

5. Sharon, Bobby, Lonny, Annette, Darlene, Cubby, Karen, and Don were all **Mouseketeers**.

6. Jiminy Cricket, Geppetto, and Monstro were all characters in *Pinocchio*.

7. Ernie, Bert, Grover, and Oscar can all be found on **"Sesame Street."**

8. Weird Harold, Mush Mouth, and Donald were all characters on **"Fat Albert & the Cosby Kids."**

9. Morticia, Gomez, Pugsley, Wednesday, and Uncle Fester were all members of **"The Addams Family."**

10. Herman, Lily, Eddie, and Marilyn were all **Munsters**.

Test Number 6: **SIMPSON MANIA**

1. Bart Simpson's favorite cartoon show is **"Itchy and Scratchy."**

2. **Smithers** is Mr. Burns's bootlicking assistant.

3. Homer does his drinking at **Moe's**.

4. **Julie Kavner**, once Rhoda's sister, performs the voice of Marge Simpson.

5. The Simpson family dog is **Santa's Little Helper**.

6. Homer drinks **Duff beer**.

7. Bart's teacher's name is **Mrs. Karbappel**.

8. Lisa plays the **saxophone**.

9. The Simpsons' next-door neighbors are the **Flanders**.

10. The creator of "The Simpsons" is cartoonist **Matt Groening**.

Test Number 7:
ONCE UPON A TIME, IN A LAND FAR, FAR AWAY . . .

1. The Flintstones live in the prehistoric city of **Bedrock**.

2. Superman (and Clark Kent) live in the city of **Metropolis**.

3. Batman (and Bruce Wayne) live in the city of **Gotham**.

4. The Simpsons live in the city of **Springfield**.

5. The Jetsons live in the **Skypad** Apartments.

Answers

6. Howdy Doody's hometown was **Doodyville**.

7. Kukla, Ollie, Fletcher Rabbit, Beulah the Witch, and Madame Ooglepuss were all **Kuklapolitans**.

8. Sky King and Penny lived at the **Flying Crown** Ranch.

9. Archie, Jughead, Veronica, Betty, and Reggie go to **Riverdale High**.

10. ALF's home planet was **Melmac**.

Test Number 8: **DISNEY IMPRESSIONS**

1. **Ludwig Von Drake** was the duck professor.

2. **Michael Eisner** is the head of the Disney Corporation.

3. The Four Lands at Disneyland are **Adventureland, Fantasyland, Frontierland**, and **Tomorrowland**.

4. **Fess Parker** played Davy Crockett in the fifties.

5. **Tim Dunigan** played Davy Crockett in the eighties.

6. *Beauty and the Beast* and *Aladdin* were the back-to-back hits for Disney animators in 1991 and 1992.

7. **Angela Lansbury** sang the title song in *Beauty and the Beast*.

8. **Robin Williams** did the voice of the genie in *Aladdin*.

9. **Huey, Louie, and Dewey** are Donald Duck's nephews.

10. The original "Absent-Minded Professor" was played by **Fred MacMurray** and **Harry Anderson** played the character in the made-for-television sequel.

All the tests we took in school made us feel bad when we didn't do well. We were ashamed of what we didn't know. In this test, you might feel a bit sheepish if you knew too much. After all, think of all the self-improvement you could have engaged in while you were sponging up all this knowledge.

Nobody has to stay after school for not doing well on this test. Nobody's going to tell your parents (though they'd probably feel better if you did a bad job on this test). But, if you knew much of the information tested in this section, then you have a good memory, and you know much about what frames the lives of so many American childhoods.

Scoring

150–201 Correct: You didn't get out enough.

100–149 Correct: TV was a consistent baby-sitter.

50–99 Correct: You had a fairly balanced childhood—a bit of TV, a bit of homework, a bit of play.

Less Than 50 Correct: You often didn't know what the other kids were talking about.

4

Tabloid Television

"The television is shadows . . . A world comes into your house—and it is shadows."

TILLIE OLSEN

Way back in the early to mid-fifties, there was a hit TV show hosted by a comedian named Red Buttons. He started a mini-fad with the song he did each week, a song that went "Ho-Ho . . . Hee-Hee . . . Ha-Ha . . . Strange Things Are Happening." Across the nation, little kids on playgrounds imitated his little dance and sang his little song. We didn't know it then, but the strangeness of the world was in the process of getting even stranger, and television itself was part of that strangeness. It not only gave us an altered way of viewing the world, where distances were shrunk and time was folded, but it also would present us with an expanded smorgasbord of the bizarre: hillbillies in mansions in Beverly Hills, martian houseguests, suburban witches, and a whole range of new creatures from Smurfs to Cookie Monsters, from talking frogs to singing pigs.

It was also a world incredibly more violent than the world we once knew, a world where nearly everyone was armed and where a killing was certain to occur at least once per half hour. By the time a viewer reached the age of eighteen, he or she had witnessed some 350,000 acts of violence.

We got used to this strange world very quickly, but, in the interest of sanity, it is useful once in a while to reflect on just how strange some of the things we got used to have become.

The test that follows is made up of strange things. If you don't think some of these things are strange, it may be that you have completely merged with the strange world of television. At a slight remove, some of what we see on television could be headline material for the tabloid press. The questions below are constructed to read like the front page of the *Star* or the *National Enquirer*. We enter into the world of fiction with the "willing suspension of disbelief." TV has made that suspension of disbelief easier and easier. If we believed this stuff, we'll believe anything. Enter now the strange world of tabloid televison.

STRANGE THINGS ARE HAPPENING!

If you watched TV, you actually saw these things. Here are the headlines. You identify the subject or the person in question.

1. Man forecasts weather while dressed as Carmen Miranda. What man? _____

2. Extraterrestrial father and earthling mother give birth to middle-aged baby. What show?_____

3. Man has fat from his buttocks injected into his forehead on national television. What man?_____

4. Neighbor drowns in bowl of chicken soup. What show?_____

5. Teenage doctor loses virginity. What show?_____

6. Man wins heart's desire with "Venus Butterfly."
    What show?_____

7. Frog pines away for the love of a pig.
    What frog?_____

8. Compulsive woman repeats the phrase "Sock it to me" each
    week. What woman?_____

9. Shoe salesman remains wedded to woman he hates.
    What man?_____

10. Man's death and burial—and an entire year of episodes—turn out
    to be nothing but bad dream.
    What show?_____

11. Newsman walks off. Eight minutes of dead air.
    What newsman?_____

12. Politician can't spell "potato." What politician?_____

13. Senators discuss *The Exorcist*, soft-drink cans, and pubic hair.
    What were they doing?_____

14. Naked man exposes his "shortcomings" before a national audi-
    ence. What event?_____

15. Woman emerges from a bottle without a navel.
    What show?_____

16. Marine landing impeded by swarms of TV cameras.
    Where?_____

17. TV host calls nation's leader a sushi puker.
    What host_____

18. Comedian makes ambiguous hand gestures. Career goes into eclipse. What comedian?_____

19. Friends hysterical over the death of a clown. What show?_____

20. Man obsessed by power tools reverts to ape. What show?_____

21. Bandleader's wife gives birth to make-believe baby and real baby at the same time. What show?_____

22. Future president plays Soviet general on *G.E. Theater*. Fictional Soviet general renounces communism. What future president?_____

23. Talk show host appears in drag. What host?_____

24. Talk show host experiences dramatic weight loss, followed by dramatic weight gain. What host?_____

25. Big-city mayor says: "The police aren't there to create disorder— the police are there to preserve disorder." What mayor?_____

26. Sports commentator says blacks are genetically disposed to be superior athletes. Commentator loses job. What commentator?_____

27. Woman with speech impediment wins multimillion-dollar broadcast contract. What woman?_____

28. Foulmouthed, overweight slattern becomes America's darling. What slattern?_____

29. L.A.P.D. staffed with aliens. What show?_____

30. Sammy Davis, Jr. visits workingman's home. Kisses bigot. What bigot?_____

31. Man drinks countless beers every day for ten years; never gets drunk. What man?_____

32. Thirty-year-old paperboy lives with his parents. What show?_____

33. TV anchorwoman irritates veep, becomes unwed mother. What unwed mother?_____

34. Man hosts teenage dance show, never ages. What man?_____

35. Talentless man conducts talent search. What man?_____

36. Aeronautically enhanced convent dweller astonishes colleagues. What convent dweller?_____

37. Man heads middle-class family without visible means of support. What man?_____

38. Anal-retentive photographer shares space with slovenly sportswriter. What show?_____

39. Black man dresses as woman, calls himself "Geraldine," claims the devil made him do it. What man?_____

40. Corporation manufactures napalm; later advertises that their company "lets you do great things."
What corporation?_____

41. Kid-show host nabbed in porn theater bust.
What host?_____

42. Ex-White House chief of staff caught in "Crossfire."
What White House Chief?_____

43. Man has two mute brothers, both with same first name.
What show?_____

44. Man's advertising career impeded by occult wife.
What man?_____

45. Evangelist caught with prostitute, weeps, begs forgiveness, repeats offense.
What evangelist?_____

46. Woman embarrassed by husband's shirts, chided for laundry deficiencies. What commercial?_____

47. Diminutive yuppie forsakes parental ideals.
What yuppie?_____

48. Land shark terrorizes New York.
What show?_____

49. Veep tells blacks "it's a terrible thing to lose one's mind."
What veep?_____

50. Mounted man in armor rides through neighborhoods cleaning clothes.
What commercial?_____

51. Homosexuals force woman out of fruit-drink job.
    What woman?_____

52. Androgynous man marries Miss Vicky on national TV. Ratings
    soar. What androgynous man?_____

53. Tiny person navigates toilet tanks.
    What commercial?_____

54. Samurai warrior goes through succession of career changes.
    What show?_____

55. Farm family supervised by hyperintelligent collie.
    What collie?_____

56. Family squabbles over frozen waffles.
    What commercial?_____

57. Fruit quartet sings praises of intimate apparel.
    What commercial?_____

58. Store owner indulges bathroom tissue fetish.
    What commercial?_____

59. Arboreal mammal knocks airline.
    What mammal?_____
    What airline?_____

60. Breakfast food talks! What commercial?_____

61. Cigarettes dance! What commercial?_____

62. Cartoon tuna with apparent death wish rejected by seafood can-
    nery.
    What commercial?_____

63. Big-city mayor's failed seduction captured on videotape.
    What mayor?_____
    What city?_____

64. Rooftop reporter dodges missiles. Dubbed "Scud Stud."
    What reporter?_____

65. Dimwit's mother reincarnated as antique vehicle.
    What show?_____

66. Wealthy teens suffer angst. What show?_____

67. Yuppies suffer angst. What show?_____

68. Game show host's hair turns white overnight.
    What host?_____

69. VP candidate turns off hearing aid during debate.
    What candidate?_____

70. Once-upon-a-time American princess touts adult diapers.
    What princess?_____

71. One CBS newsman ejected from Democratic convention, another
    roughed up on the floor.
    What newsmen?_____

72. Celebrity-for-life slaps Beverly Hills cop.
    What celebrity?_____

73. First Lady's father makes appearance in a sitcom.
    Whose father?_____

74. Big-eared candidate says he's "all ears."
    What candidate?_____

75. Friends wager on who can abstain from masturbation the longest.
What show?_____

76. Microscopic sea monkeys blown up to human size by mad scientist.
What kid show? _____

77. Singing policemen, singing lawyers, singing judges.
What show?_____

78. Man has four-part head made up of angel, animal, wimp, and genius—the parts talk, and we can see them.
What show?_____

79. Performer signs off each show with the enigmatic "Good night, Mrs. Calabash, wherever you are."
What performer?_____

STRANGE THINGS ARE HAPPENING!

1. Man forecasts weather as Carmen Miranda: **Willard Scott**

2. Extraterrestrial father and earthling mother give birth to middle-aged baby: **"Mork and Mindy"**

3. Man has fat from his buttocks injected into his forehead: **Geraldo Rivera**

4. Neighbor drowns in soup: **"Mary Hartman, Mary Hartman"**

5. Teenage doctor loses virginity: **"Doogie Howser, M.D."**

6. Man wins heart's desire with "Venus Butterfly": **"L.A. Law"**

7. Frog pines away for the love of a pig: **Kermit**

8. Compulsive woman repeats the phrase "Sock it to me": **Judy Carne**

9. Shoe salesman remains wedded to woman he hates: **Al Bundy**

10. Man's death and burial—and an entire year of episodes—turn out to be nothing but bad dream: **"Dallas"**

11. Newsman walks off. Eight minutes of dead air: **Dan Rather**

12. Politician can't spell "potato": **Dan Quayle**

13. Senators discuss *The Exorcist*, soft-drink cans, and pubic hair: **Supreme Court confirmation hearings**

14. Naked man exposes his "shortcomings" before a national audience: **Academy Awards**

15. Woman emerges from a bottle without a navel: **"I Dream of Jeannie"**

Answers

16. Marine landing impeded by swarms of TV cameras: **Somalia**

17. TV host calls nation's leader a sushi puker: **Arsenio Hall**

18. Comedian makes ambiguous hand gestures: **Jackie Mason**

19. Friends hysterical over the death of a clown: **"The Mary Tyler Moore Show"**

20. Man obsessed by power tools: **"Home Improvement"**

21. Bandleader's wife gives birth: **"I Love Lucy"**

22. Future president plays Soviet general: **Ronald Reagan**

23. Talk show host appears in drag: **Phil Donahue**

24. Talk show host experiences dramatic weight loss: **Oprah Winfrey**

25. Big-city mayor says: "The police aren't there to create disorder—the police are there to preserve disorder": **Mayor Richard Daley**

26. Sports commentator says blacks are genetically disposed to be superior athletes: **Jimmy "the Greek" Snyder**

27. Woman with speech impediment: **Barbara Walters**

28. Foulmouthed, overweight slattern becomes America's darling: **Roseanne Barr/Arnold**

29. L.A.P.D. staffed with aliens: **"Alien Nation"**

30. Sammy Davis, Jr. visits workingman's home. Kisses bigot:
Archie Bunker

31. Man drinks countless beers every day for ten years; never gets drunk: **Norm Peterson**

32. Thirty-year-old paperboy lives with his parents: **"Get a Life"**

33. TV anchorwoman irritates veep, becomes unwed mother:
Murphy Brown

34. Man hosts teenage dance show: **Dick Clark**

35. Talentless man conducts talent search: **Ed McMahon**

36. Aeronautically enhanced convent dweller astonishes colleagues:
Sister Bertrille on "The Flying Nun"

37. Man heads middle-class family without visible means of support:
Ozzie Nelson

38. Anal-retentive photographer shares space with slovenly sports-writer: **"The Odd Couple"**

39. Black man dresses as woman, calls himself "Geraldine":
Flip Wilson

40. Corporation manufactures napalm: **Dow Chemical**

41. Kid-show host nabbed in porn theater bust: **Pee Wee Herman**

42. Ex-White House chief of staff caught in
"Crossfire": **John Sununu**

43. Man has two mute brothers: **"Newhart"**

Answers

44. Man's advertising career impeded by occult wife: **Darrin Stevens**

45. Evangelist caught with prostitute, weeps, begs forgiveness, repeats offense: **Jimmy Swaggart**

46. Woman embarrassed by husband's shirts: **Wisk**

47. Diminutive yuppie forsakes parental ideals: **Alex Keaton**

48. Land shark terrorizes New York: **"Saturday Night Live"**

49. Veep tells blacks "it's a terrible thing to lose one's mind": **Dan Quayle**

50. Mounted man in armor rides through neighborhoods cleaning clothes: **Ajax**

51. Homosexuals force woman out of fruit-drink job: **Anita Bryant**

52. Androgynous man marries Miss Vicky on national TV: **Tiny Tim**

53. Tiny person navigates toilet tanks: **Tidy Bowl**

54. Samurai warrior goes through succession of career changes: **"Saturday Night Live"**

55. Farm family supervised by hyperintelligent collie: **Lassie**

56. Family squabbles over frozen waffles: **Eggo**

57. Fruit quartet sings praises of intimate apparel: **Fruit of the Loom**

58. Store owner indulges bathroom tissue fetish: **Charmin**

59. Mammal: **Koala bear** Airline: **Quantas**

60. Breakfast food talks!: **Rice Krispies**

61. Cigarettes dance!: **Old Gold**

62. Cartoon tuna with apparent death wish rejected by seafood cannery: **Starkist**

63. Mayor: **Marion Barry** City: **Washington, D.C.**

64. Dubbed the "Scud Stud": **Arthur Kent**

65. Dimwit's mother reincarnated as antique vehicle: **"My Mother the Car"**

66. Wealthy teens suffer angst: **"Beverly Hills, 90210"**

67. Yuppies suffer angst: **"thirtysomething"**

68. Game show host's hair turns white: **Bob Barker**

69. VP candidate turns off hearing aid during debate: **Admiral James Stockdale**

70. Once-upon-a-time American Princess: **June Allyson**

71. Roughed up on the floor: **Dan Rather**
    Ejected from Demo convention: **Mike Wallace**

72. Celebrity-for-life slaps Beverly Hills cop: **Zsa Zsa Gabor**

73. First Lady's father makes appearance in a sitcom: **Hillary Clinton**

74. Big-eared candidate says he's "all ears": **H. Ross Perot**

75. Friends wager on who can abstain from masturbation the longest: **"Seinfeld"**

76. Microscopic sea monkeys blown up to human size by mad scientist: **"The Amazing Sea Monkeys"**

77. Singing policemen, singing lawyers, singing judges: **"Cop Rock"**

78. Man has four-part head made up of angel, animal, wimp, and genius: **"Herman's Head"**

79. Performer signs off each show with the enigmatic "Good night, Mrs. Calabash, wherever you are": **Jimmy Durante**

Well, was that strange, or what? My guess is that you had little trouble identifying this strangeness, however. How many of these questions did you know? This test is sort of a pass/fail kind of deal.

Scoring

40–79 Correct: You live in a strange TV world, and you know it.

0–39 Correct: The fewer you knew, the more disoriented you must be.

5

Generational TV

*"If you had that intimate a knowledge of Shakespeare, you'd
be considered a genius."*

DR. ROBERT THOMPSON, COMPARING STUDENT
KNOWLEDGE OF "THE BRADY BUNCH" TO
THEIR KNOWLEDGE OF SHAKESPEARE.

You'll find two tests here, one for those under the age of thirty, and
another for those over forty. Age before beauty; we'll begin with
what older folks are more likely to know.

Test Number 1:
TWENTY-FIVE QUESTIONS ABOUT TELEVISION YOU PROBABLY CAN'T ANSWER IF YOU'RE UNDER THIRTY

This is a challenge offered to people under thirty. Chances are, most
everything on this test came along—and faded away— before you were
born. If you would like to know why your parents are so weird, this little

test might explain some of that. Even though you weren't around for much of this stuff, I'll bet some of it has found its way into your memory bank anyway. And for those of us over thirty, this is just a brief trip down memory lane.

1. What are "rabbit ears"? _____

2. What was "Maypo"? _____

3. On what show would you have heard the question, "Is it bigger than a bread box?" _____

4. Who played Davy Crockett's sidekick in Disney's "Adventures of Davy Crockett"? _____

5. Who was Topo Gigio? _____

6. Who played the title role in the series "December Bride"? _____

7. Complete this advertising slogan: "Poof! There goes _____."

8. "Sugarfoot," "Cheyenne," and "Maverick" were all westerns made by what studio? _____

9. "Point of order, point of order" was a phrase heard in early televised Senate hearings.
What is the phrase associated with? _____

10. In the fifties, there were four major networks: NBC, CBS, ABC, and _____ .

11. What was the name of "The Ed Sullivan Show" before it was called "The Ed Sullivan Show"? _____

12. He was the most famous (and notorious) of the cheaters in the quiz show scandals of the 1950s. His first name was Charles; what was his last name? _____

13. Uncle Miltie was the first TV mega star. Who sponsored his popular show? _____

14. He was the most famous of the wrestlers on fifties TV. What was his name? _____

15. Name the school where "Our Miss Brooks" taught.

_____

16. He first came to our attention as the comedian with "the button-down mind." _____

17. What product did Betty Furness promote on fifties television? _____

18. "Sing Along With _____." Who?

19. The sponsor most associated with Arthur Godfrey was

_____ .

20. Jonathan Winter's character, Maude _____ .

21. Art Linkletter segments: "People Are _____"
and "Kids Say the _____ ."

22. a. Complete the following phrase: "All things were as they were then, except _____ ."
b. Who spoke those words and introduced the series?_____

23. "American Bandstand" was originally broadcast from
what city? _____

24. The schoolmistress on "Ding Dong School" was _____

25. Fifties TV staples: a. _____ Neff,
    b. Sir Cedric _____ ,   c. _____ Bendix,
    d. _____ Lescoulie,   e. Snooky _____ ,
    f. Julius _____ ,   g. Carmel _____ .

Test Number 2:

TWENTY-FIVE QUESTIONS ABOUT TELEVISION YOU PROBABLY CAN'T ANSWER IF YOU'RE OVER FORTY

You know how younger people delight in making you feel hopelessly out of it? This is some of the stuff that allows them to do that.

Younger people either are watching some of these things now or they watched it when they were in their formative years, while those of us over forty were trying to be adults.

What will it prove if you flunk this test? That you're over forty, perhaps. Or that you don't watch television. Or that you're a young person who doesn't pay attention to what a lot of other young people pay attention to. Does that make you a bad person? No way. Way.

1. What are Wayne and Garth likely to say when something good happens to them? _____

2. Jason Priestly, Shannen Doherty, Jennie Garth, and Luke Perry are all members of the cast of _____.

3. Nirvana and Pearl Jam. What city are they from? _____

4. What does Arsenio Hall call the band on his show? _____

5. Max Headroom was on fictional Channel _____.

6. Teenage pyromaniacs whose primary vocabulary is limited to the words "cool" amd "sucks" _____

7. Fill in the blanks: "Tonight on MTV.
The Red Hot _____."

8. She tore up a picture of the pope on "Saturday Night Live." _____

9. Which of the following *is not* a rock or rap group? a. Arrested Development; b. Temple of the Dog; c. Faith No More; d. Hole; e.Quivering Meat; f. Jesus Jones; g. Meat Puppets _____

10. What are X-Men? _____

11. Mrs. Brady's nephew came to stay with the Bradys.
What was his name? _____

12. Who played the nanny on "Nanny and the Professor"? _____

13. Scooby Doo's human sidekick was named _____.

14. Sharon Stone (of *Basic Instinct* notoriety) had a small part in a short-lived early eighties series starring Michael Nouri.
Can you name that series? _____

15. "Love Shack." Whose song and video? _____

16. What was the name of Madonna's first video? _____

17. Among the first VJs on MTV:
a. _____ Goodman,   b. _____ Blackwood,
c. Martha _____ ,   d. J. J._____ .

18. Pauly Shore's movie debut._____

19. It was an early video seen on MTV called "China Girl." Who was the artist?_____

20. In what company would one have found "Ed Grimley"?_____

21. Cable channel VH-1: What does the VH stand for?_____

22. Who played Tabitha on the "Bewitched" spin-off?_____

23. The Fonz met his match in this woman. What was the character's name?_____

24. Her little sister, Leather, was played by rocker _____.

25. On "What's Happening," how did Raj answer the phone?_____

Answers

1. Rabbit ears are **indoor television antennas.**

2. Maypo is a **brand of hot cereal.**

3. "Is it bigger than a bread box?" was a question heard regularly on **"Art Linkletter's House Party."**

4. Davy Crockett's sidekick was **Buddy Ebsen.**

5. Topo Gigio was **an Italian mouse often seen on "The Ed Sullivan Show."**

6. **Spring Byington** was the star of "December Bride."

7. "Poof! There goes **perspiration.**"

8. "Sugarfoot," "Cheyenne," and "Maverick" were all made by **Warner Brothers.**

9. "Point of order, point of order" was a phrase associated with the **Army/McCarthy hearings.**

10. The four major networks in the fiftiess were NBC, CBS, ABC, and **DuMont.**

11. Before it was called "The Ed Sullivan Show," it was called **"The Toast of the Town."**

12. The most famous (and notorious) of the cheaters in the quiz show scandals of the 1950s was Charles **Van Doren.**

13. Uncle Miltie was sponsored by **Texaco.**

14. The most famous wrestler on fifties TV was **Gorgeous George.**

15. "Our Miss Brooks" taught at **Madison High School.**

16. **Bob Newhart** was the comedian with "the button-down mind."

17. Betty Furness sold **refrigerators** on fifties television.

18. It was "Sing Along With **Mitch,**" for Mitch Miller.

19. Arthur Godfrey's sponsor was **Lipton.**

20. Jonathan Winter's character was Maude **Frickert.**

21. The Art Linkletter segments were "People Are **Funny**" and "Kids Say the **Darnedest Things.**"

22. a. "All things were as they were then, except **you are there.**"
b. **Walter Cronkite** spoke those words, and introduced the series, called "You Are There."

23. "American Bandstand" was originally broadcast from **Philadelphia.**

24. The schoolmistress on "Ding Dong School" was **Miss Francis.**

25. Fifties TV staples: a. **Hildegard** Neff, b. Sir Cedric **Hardwicke,** c. **William** Bendix, d. **Jack** Lescoulie, e. Snooky **Lanson,** f. Julius **LaRosa,** g. Carmel **Quinn.**

Scoring : If you missed most of these, you're either losing your memory, or this stuff was way before your time.

Answers

1. Wayne and Garth say **"Excellent"** or **"We're Not Worthy."**

2. Jason Priestly, Shannen Doherty, Jennie Garth, and Luke Perry are all members of the cast of **"Beverly Hills, 90210."**

3. Nirvana and Pearl Jam are from **Seattle.**

4. Arsenio Hall calls the band his **posse.**

5. Max Headroom was on fictional Channel **23.**

6. **Beavis** and **Butthead** think things are either "cool" or that they "suck."

7. The Red Hot **Chili Peppers** appear on MTV.

8. **Sinead O'Connor** tore up a picture of the Pope.

9. **(e) Quivering Meat** is not a rock or rap group.

10. X-Men are **Marvel comics superheroes and cartoon super-heroes.**

11. Mrs. Brady's nephew was **Oliver.**

12. **Juliette Mills** played the nanny on "Nanny and the Professor."

13. Scooby Doo's human sidekick was named **Shaggy.**

14. Sharon Stone had a small part in **"Bay City Blues."**

15. "Love Shack" was a hit for the **B-52s.**

16. **"Burning Up"** was Madonna's first video.

17. Among the first VJs on MTV were **Mark** Goodman, **Nina** Blackwood, Martha **Quinn**, and J. J. **Jackson.**

18. Pauly Shore's movie debut was *Encino Man*.

19. "China Girl" was by **David Bowie.**

20. "Ed Grimley" was seen on **"SCTV"** and **"Saturday Night Live."**

21. Cable channel VH-1 is **Video Hits 1.**

22. **Lisa Hartman** played Tabitha on the "Bewitched" spin-off.

23. The Fonz met his match in **Pinky Tuscadero.**

24. Leather was played by **Suzi Quatro.**

25. Raj answered the phone saying, **"Which Doobie You Be?"**

Scoring : If you didn't know at least half of these, then you're probably on the downslope of 40.

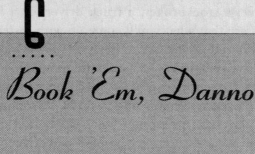

Book 'Em, Danno

**THE COUCH POTATO'S GUIDE
TO COPS, DICKS,
GUMSHOES, AND P.I.s.**

*"One of television's great contributions is that it brought
murder back into the home, where it belongs."*
ALFRED HITCHCOCK

*"If you think of television programming as an All-American
menu, then the detective show is definitely the hamburger."*
MARTHA BOYLES

According to the most recent research, an American child witnesses some eight thousand simulated video murders by the time his or her elementary school years are complete. Researchers tallying a single day's broadcasting in our nation's capital counted 1,846 violent acts in that single broadcast day. Not all of this violence, murder, and mayhem are found on the cop shows, of course; a goodly proportion is to be found in cartoons. Still, our fascination with cops, robbers, private eyes, and assorted bad guys is nearly obsessional. No occupation, not even doctors, has been so visible through the history of television. You can flick the remote endlessly in search of a social worker, a marketing executive, a stockbroker, a truck driver, or a factory worker, but the chances are that what you'll come up with instead is a slew of homicide inspectors and private eyes.

We have seen rivers of blood and mountains of corpses, and still our appetites have not been sated. Each new television season brings new shows, recycled old plots in glitzy new surroundings. TV network execs and writers have given us wheelchair-bound detectives, hippie detectives, geriatric detectives, rumpled detectives, and sartorially resplendent detectives. We've had husband-and-wife crime busters, ecclesiastical sleuths, hard-boiled ex-con crime fighters, and postmenopausal masterminds of murder.

They've been a staple of television since the very beginning. In 1948, television offered us "Barney Blake, Police Reporter," who not only wrote about crimes, but solved them, too. NBC claims that this was the very first mystery series on television.

Who says we don't learn anything from television? Unless you're a cop, a criminal, or a lawyer, you probably learned most of what you know in the following tests from what you saw on the tube.

Test Number 1: CLASSICAL KNOWLEDGE

Who says you don't know Latin?

For the sake of verisimilitude, TV writers like to sprinkle a little technical jargon in their scripts. In the following test, we'll see if you've picked up on these legal and forensic terms so often heard on the cop shows.

1. rigor mortis _____

2. corpus delicti _____

3. habeas corpus _____

4. non compos mentis _____

5. flagrante delicto _____

6. modus operandi (m.o.) _____

7. in camera _____

8. in curia _____

9. pro bono _____

10. quid pro quo _____

Test Number 2: DRUG PARLANCE

Lamentably, our society is saddled with a serious drug problem. TV mirrors that problem. TV cops have been doing battle with drugs as far back as Jack Webb's "Dragnet." Along the way, these shows have kept us up on the language of the drug culture. Chances are, you first heard many of the following slang terms on television. Do you know their meanings?

1. a dime bag _____

2. a key _____

3. a narc _____

4. a mule _____

5. fix _____

6. works _____

7. crack house _____

8. toot, blow _____

9. speed, crank _____

10. o.d. _____

Test Number 3: ASSORTED CRIMES, CRIMINALS, AND TOOLS OF THE TRADE

Apparently, we love the tough talk of detectives and private eyes. We love the glimpses, however phony, into the underworld. That underworld comes with its own vocabulary. You can't know what's happening on TV without a working knowledge of most of the following.

1. john _____

2. fence _____

3. second-story man _____

4. piece _____

5. trick _____

6. shakedown _____

7. wise guy _____

8. soldier _____

9. stoolie _____

10. "hot" merchandise _____

Test Number 4: **PHRASES**

From the preceding general questions, we'll turn to specific shows. Like other TV genres, cop shows have given us certain repeated phrases that we associate with specific programs or characters. On what shows did we routinely hear the following phrases?

1. "Just the facts, ma'am." _____

2. "Book 'em, Danno." _____

3. "And hey, let's be careful out there." _____

4. "Just a cup of coffee and a piece of that great cherry pie."
_____

5. "Who loves ya, baby?" _____

6. "Ten-four." _____

7. "Works for me." _____

8. "There are eight million stories in the Naked City."
_____

9. "The weekly nationwide criminal manhunt." _____

10. "The story you are about to hear is true; only the names have been changed to protect the innocent." _____

We'll change the test format a bit here, and make it easier. If you've been a regular viewer of crime shows, then you'll probably be able to match the star with the series.

1. Lee Marvin _____   a. "Hill Street Blues"

2. Burt Reynolds _____   b. "Banacek"

3. Raymond Burr _____   c. "Highway Patrol"

4. Howard Duff _____   d. "Ironside"

5. Daniel J. Travanti _____ e. "Vega$"

6. Telly Savalas _____   f. "Baretta"

7. Johnny Depp _____   g. "The Commish"

8. David Janssen _____   h. "Bronk"

9. Broderick Crawford _____ i. "The Detectives"

10. Robert Urich _____   j. "T.J. Hooker"

11. George Peppard _____   k. "Racket Squad"

12. Jack Palance _____   l. "Serpico"

13. Michael Chiklis _____   m. "Streets of San Francisco"

14. Robert Taylor _____   n. "Tenspeed and Brown Shoe"

15. Robert Blake _____   o. "21 Jump Street"

16. William Shatner _____   p. "Harry-O"

17. Ben Vereen _____   q. "Kojak"

18. Reed Hadley _____   r. "M Squad"

19. David Birney _____   s. "Felony Squad"

20. Karl Malden _____   t. "Dan August"

Test Number 6: LADIES ONLY

Women fight crime, too. Match the actress to her series.

1. Helen Hayes _____   a. "Police Woman"

2. Angela Lansbury _____   b. "Mod Squad"

3. Angie Dickinson _____   c. "Get Christie Love"

4. Tyne Daly _____   d. "Honey West"

5. Cybill Shepherd _____   e. "The Avengers"

6. Tanya Roberts _____   f. " Murder, She Wrote"

7.   Peggy Lipton _____   g. "Cassie & Company"

8.   Teresa Graves _____   h. "The Snoop Sisters"

9.   Diana Rigg _____   i. "Charlie's Angels"

10. Anne Francis _____   j. "Cagney & Lacey"

                                   k. "Moonlighting"

Test Number 7: **PARTNERS IN CRIME FIGHTING**

There are the lone crime fighters, and then there are those who team up. When they team up, the writers often name the show after them. There have been lots of these pairings. Do you know the ones in this little quiz?

Fill in the blanks.

1. MacGruder and _____

2. Starsky and _____

3. Tequila and _____

4. McMillan and _____

5. Tenspeed and _____

6. Pros and _____ (also known as "Gabriel's Fire")

7. B.J. and _____

8. Simon and _____

9. Jake and _____

10. Scarecrow and _____

Test Number 8: GIMMICKS

It's the hook, the thing to get our attention, the little bit of superficial characterization that is meant to set one TV character apart from all the others. But we're not fooled; we know a gimmick when we see one.

1. He fought crime, but a cockatoo was his best friend._____

2. He fought crime, but he enjoyed his lollipop._____

3. He fought crime, but he was also a tough-guy priest with a pal named One Ball._____

4. He fought crime in his rumpled raincoat._____

5. He fought crime, but in his off-hours he hung out at a jazz club called Mother's. _____

6. She fought crime, but writing mystery novels was what put groceries in the cupboard of her Maine home._____

7. He fought crime, but he was very old._____

8. He fought crime, but he was very fat._____

9. He fought crime, but he was confined to a wheelchair._____

10. They fought crime in Florida, but they dressed very well and had nice cars._____

11. They fought crime with the help of Huggy Bear._____

12. He fought crime, but he lived in a trailer._____

13. They fought crime, but these two women often fought with each other as well. _____

14. He fought crime, but he was Polish-American. _____

15. He fought crime, especially Wo Fat. _____

16. He fought crime with the help of his Number 1 son. _____

17. He fought crime, but he drove a Ferrari and lived in Hawaii. _____

18. He fought crime, but he was a recovering alcoholic who had a romantic relationship with a public defense lawyer. _____

19. They fought crime, with occasional help from a vain parking lot attendant who was always combing his hair. _____

20. He fought crime with the help of Ozzie the Answer, and Jenny, the bartender at Light n' Easy. _____

21. He fought crime down south, with the help of a black chief of detectives named Tibbs. _____

22. He fought crime in his KITT, a talking car. _____

23. He fought crime, especially Frank Nitti. _____

24. He fought crime, but he got his messages from "Sam" at his answering service. _____

25. They fight "bad boys," but they're the real thing. _____

26. He fought crime (one of the first to do so on TV), but he was only an "enemy to those who make him an enemy, a friend to those who have no friend." _____

27. They are brothers, they fight crime, and they get help from "Downtown" Brown. _____

28. They fight crime, and they all wear hats. _____

29. They fought crime in the L.A. schools because they could pass for students. _____

30. She fought crime, and her nickname was "Pepper." (Sgt. Pepper, to you.) _____

TWO LITTLE BONUS QUESTIONS

Anything so formula-ridden and gimmicky as the cop/detective genre is bound to attract satire and inspire takeoffs. And there have been plenty. Remember these?

1. Frank Drebin wasn't like all those super-competent cops. He was on _____.

2. With his .44 Magnum he affectionately called "Gun," this guy was a danger to himself and others. He was Inspector _____.

Test Number 1: CLASSICAL KNOWLEDGE

Answers

1. rigor mortis: **the stiffness seen in corpses**

2. corpus delicti: **the body of a murder victim and the facts substantiating that a murder occurred**

3. habeas corpus: **an order that a detained person be brought before a court to determine the legality of his detention**

4. non compos mentis: **mentally incompetent**

5. flagrante delicto: **caught in the act**

6. modus operandi (m.o.): **method of operation**

7. in camera: **in the judge's chambers**

8. in curia: **in court**

9. pro bono: **when a lawyer represents someone without charge**

10. quid pro quo: **a fair exchange**

Test Number 2: DRUG PARLANCE

1. a dime bag: **a $10 supply of drugs, usually marijuana**

2. a key: **a kilo, or kilogram**

3. a narc: **a narcotics law enforcement officer, usually undercover**

4. a mule: **a drug courier**

5. fix: **an injection of a narcotic by an addict**

6. works: **drug paraphernalia**

7. crack house: **a place from which crack cocaine is dealt or consumed**

8. toot, blow: **cocaine**

9. speed, crank: **amphetamines/uppers**

10. o.d.: **overdose**

Test Number 3: ASSORTED CRIMES, CRIMINALS, AND TOOLS OF THE TRADE

1. john: **a prostitute's client**

2. fence: **a buyer/seller of stolen goods**

3. second-story man: **a burglar**

4. piece: **a gun**

5. trick: **a john or the services provided to him**

6. shakedown: **extortion/blackmail**

7. wise guy: **a gangster**

8. soldier: **in underworld parlance, an enforcer, triggerman; one of the rank-and-file mobsters**

9. stoolie: **a stool pigeon/informer**

10. "hot" merchandise: **stolen goods**

Test Number 4: **PHRASES**

1. "Just the facts, ma'am": **"Dragnet"**

2. "Book 'em, Danno": **"Hawaii Five-O"**

3. "And hey, let's be careful out there": **"Hill Street Blues"**

4. "Just a cup of coffee and a piece of that great cherry pie": **"Twin Peaks"**

5. "Who loves ya, baby?": **"Kojak"**

6. "Ten-four": **"Highway Patrol"**

7. "Works for me": **"Hunter"**

8. "There are eight million stories in the Naked City" : **"Naked City"**

9. "The weekly nationwide criminal manhunt": **"America's Most Wanted"**

10. "The story you are about to hear is true": **"Dragnet"**

Test Number 5: **MIX AND MATCH**

1. Lee Marvin: **(r) "M Squad"**

2. Burt Reynolds: **(t) "Dan August"**

3. Raymond Burr: **(d) "Ironside"**

4. Howard Duff: **(s) "Felony Squad"**

5. Daniel J. Travanti: **(a) "Hill Street Blues"**

6. Telly Savalas: **(q) "Kojak"**

7. Johnny Depp: **(o) "21 Jump Street"**

8. David Janssen; **(p) "Harry-O"**

9. Broderick Crawford: **(c) "Highway Patrol"**

10. Robert Urich: **(e) "Vega$"**

11. George Peppard: **(b) "Banacek"**

12. Jack Palance: **(h) "Bronk"**

13. Michael Chiklis: **(g) "The Commish"**

14. Robert Taylor: **(i) "The Detectives"**

15. Robert Blake: **(f) "Baretta"**

16. William Shatner: **(j) "T.J. Hooker"**

17. Ben Vereen: **(n) "Tenspeed and Brown Shoe"**

18. Reed Hadley: **(k) "Racket Squad"**

19. David Birney: **(l) "Serpico"**

20. Karl Malden: **(m) "Streets of San Francisco"**

Test Number 6: LADIES ONLY

Answers

1. Helen Hayes: **(h) "The Snoop Sisters"**

2. Angela Lansbury: **(f) "Murder, She Wrote"**

3. Angie Dickinson: **(a) "Police Woman"** and **(g) "Cassie & Company"**

4. Tyne Daly: **(j) "Cagney & Lacey"**

5. Cybill Shepherd: **(k) "Moonlighting"**

6. Tanya Roberts: **(i) "Charlie's Angels"**

7. Peggy Lipton: **(b) "Mod Squad"**

8. Teresa Graves: **(c) "Get Christie Love"**

9. Diana Rigg: **(e) "The Avengers"**

10. Anne Francis: **(d) "Honey West"**

Test Number 7: PARTNERS IN CRIME FIGHTING

1. "MacGruder and **Loud**"

2. "Starsky and **Hutch**"

3. "Tequila and **Bonetti**"

4. "McMillan and **Wife**"

5. "Tenspeed and **Brown Shoe**"

6. "Pros and **Cons**"

7. "B.J. and **the Bear**"

8. "Simon and **Simon**"

9. "Jake and **the Fatman**"

10. "Scarecrow and **Mrs. King**"

Test Number 8: **GIMMICKS**

1. He fought crime, but a cockatoo was his best friend: **Tony Baretta**

2. He fought crime, but he enjoyed his lollipop: **Theo Kojak**

3. He fought crime, but he was also a tough-guy priest: **Father "Hardstep" Rivers** on "Hell Town"

4. He fought crime in his rumpled raincoat: **Lt. Columbo**

5. He fought crime, but in his off-hours he hung out at a jazz club called Mother's: **Peter Gunn**

6. She fought crime, but writing mystery novels was what put groceries in the cupboard of her Maine home: **Jessica Fletcher** on "Murder, She Wrote"

7. He fought crime, but he was very old: **Barnaby Jones**

8. He fought crime, but he was very fat: **J. L. McCabe** on "Jake and the Fatman"

9. He fought crime, but he was confined to a wheelchair: **Robert Ironside**

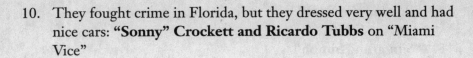

10. They fought crime in Florida, but they dressed very well and had nice cars: **"Sonny" Crockett and Ricardo Tubbs** on "Miami Vice"

11. They fought crime with the help of Huggy Bear: **Dave Starsky and Ken Hutchinson** on "Starsky and Hutch"

12. He fought crime, but he lived in a trailer: **Jim Rockford**

13. They fought crime, but these two women often fought with each other as well: **Chris Cagney and Mary Beth Lacey**

14. He fought crime, but he was Polish-American: **Thomas Banacek**

15. He fought crime, especially Wo Fat: **Steve McGarrett** on "Hawaii Five-O"

16. He fought crime with the help of his Number 1 son: **Charlie Chan**

17. He fought crime and drove a Ferrari: **Thomas Magnum**

18. He fought crime, but he was a recovering alcoholic who had a romantic relationship with a public defense lawyer: **Frank Furillo** on "Hill Street Blues"

19. They fought crime, with occasional help from a vain parking lot attendant: **Stu Bailey and Jeff Spencer** on "77 Sunset Strip"

20. He fought crime with the help of Ozzie the Answer, and Jenny, the bartender at Light n' Easy: **Mike Hammer**

21. He fought crime down south, with the help of a black chief of detectives named Tibbs: **Bill Gillespie** on "In the Heat of the Night"

22. He fought crime in KITT: **Michael Knight** on "Knight Rider"

23. He fought crime, especially Frank Nitti: **Eliot Ness** on "The Untouchables"

24. He fought crime, but he got his messages from "Sam": **Richard Diamond**

25. They fight "bad boys": **"Cops"**

26. He fought crime, but he was only an "enemy to those who make him an enemy": **Boston Blackie**

27. They are brothers, and get help from "Downtown" Brown: **A. J. Simon and Rick Simon**

28. They all wear hats: **The Hat Squad**

29. They fought crime, but they passed for students: **Tom Hanson, Judy Hoffs,** and **Harry Truman Ioki** on "21 Jump Street"

30. She fought crime, and her nickname was "Pepper": **Suzanne Anderson** on "Police Woman"

TWO LITTLE BONUS QUESTIONS

1. Frank Drebin was on **"Police Squad."**

2. The guy with the .44 Magnum was **Sledge Hammer** (and the gags were usually about as subtle).

That wraps up this case. Were you able to follow the clues to find the answers?

There were 112 questions in this test. You already have a pretty good idea of how you did, because if you made it this far, you were probably doing pretty well.

Scoring

75–112 Correct: Ace detective, and avid cop watcher.

50–74 Correct: You may yet make lieutenant.

25–49 Correct: Still a beat cop.

0–24 Correct: You haven't made the force yet.

7

Return With Us Now

"If the television craze continues with this level of programs, we are destined to become a nation of morons."
                                           DANIEL MARSH, 1950

Were you a fan of westerns? Did you read Louis L'Amour and wait anxiously for each new episode of "Gunsmoke"? Did you follow the exploits of Robert Duvall and Tommy Lee Jones as they took the herd from Lonesome Dove to Montana? Do you remember seeing Lloyd Bridges in a mid-sixties series called "The Loner"? Even now, when you're channel surfing with the remote control, are you more likely to stop when you see men on horseback?

During the 1959–60 television season, there were thirty westerns on prime time. By 1965, that number had dwindled to just seven. In the 1990s, westerns are hard to find, even in reruns, though you can usually get a "Gunsmoke" or "Bonanza" fix if you really need one. There just don't seem to be as many of us western fans as there once were.

Who knows why the late fifties and early sixties were a time when westerns were so popular? Perhaps, in that era of conformity and the growth of vast and faceless corporations, we hungered for the individual hero. Maybe we were attracted to the apparent simplicity of an earlier time when, it seemed, moral judgments were not so murky, when good guys and bad guys were easily distinguished. And who knows why the popularity of westerns declined so precipitously? Did we outgrow them? Were they too expensive to make? Had we lost touch with the mythology of our national past?

But 1992 saw a significant contribution to the western genre when Clint Eastwood, a TV western star, brought us *Unforgiven*. Perhaps the success of that film will reawaken interest in westerns. In the meantime, we'll have to make do with reruns, and memories.

So saddle up, and return with us now to those thrilling days of yesteryear. (Where have you heard that line before, anyway?)

Test Number 1: **ONCE UPON A TIME IN THE WEST**

Identify the following stars who got their careers started on television westerns.

1. First he fought "The Blob," then he was bounty hunter Josh Randall. _____

2. Before M*A*S*H, he starred in a series called "Stagecoach." _____

3. He was a gambler named Bret, with a brother named Bart, on a show called "Maverick." _____

4. She played Audra Barkley, Barbara Stanwyck's daughter on "The Big Valley." _____

5. He was lawman Hoby Gilman on "Trackdown" before teaming up with Bill Cosby in a landmark sixties series. _____

6. He was half-breed blacksmith Quint Asper on "Gunsmoke." _____

7. He played Cousin Beauregard Maverick before being "Bonded." _____

8. He first came to general attention as Shane, in the short-lived series of the same name. _____

9. He's perhaps best remembered for the role of Paladin on "Have Gun Will Travel," but he was a noted stage and screen actor as well. _____

10. First he was a teenage werewolf, then he was Little Joe. _____

Test Number 2: **LAST NAMES**

1. On "Gunsmoke," Dennis Weaver played Chester _____ , Milburn Stone played Doc _____ , and Ken Curtis played Festus _____ .

2. On "The Big Valley," Barbara Stanwyck was the matriarch of the _____ family.

3. Easy question. Ben, Hoss, Little Joe, and Adam were all members of the _____ family.

4. The trail boss on "Rawhide" was Gil _____ .

5. Lee Horsley played Ethan _____
on "Paradise."

6. Leif Erickson played Big John, the patriarch of the_____
clan on "The High Chaparral."

7. Scott Brady played Shotgun _____
in the 1959–61 series of the same name.

8. On "The Wild, Wild West," Robert Conrad played
James T. _____.

9. Father and son Lucas and Mark were the main characters in
"The Rifleman." What was their last name? _____

10. On "The Young Riders," Stephen Baldwin plays young Billy
_____ and Josh Brolin plays young Jimmy
_____ , not-yet-famous heroes of the old West.

Test Number 3: **SOMEWHERE IN THE WEST**

Though many western heroes were drifters, some of them were rooted
in particular places. Since setting is important in westerns, this is a little
test of the more famous settings. In what towns or places were the following westerns set?

1. An easy one, for starters. Matt, Kitty, Doc, Chester, and Festus
were all residents of _____,
_____ . (The town *and* the state, please.)

2. Paladin was based in this city. _____

3. In what mountain range would you find the Ponderosa ranch?
_____

4. Lonesome Dove was a border place. On one side of the border was _____ and on the other side was

_____ .

5. "The Big Valley" was set in a real valley. What valley? _____ In what state? _____

6. The Cannon family fought Apaches on "The High Chaparral." At the time, it was a territory, but it would become the state of

_____ .

7. "The Young Riders" features the fictional exploits of Pony Express riders. Historically, the Pony Express connected _____ , Missouri, with _____ , California.

8. It was "the town too tough to die," both in reality, and in this fifties series entitled "_____ Territory."

9. 20 Mule Team Borax sponsored this show, set in the valley where borax was mined. What valley? _____

10. The name of the town where "The Rifleman" and his son lived was _____ .

Test Number 4: **WHO WAS THAT MASKED MAN, ANYWAY?**

The following questions all concern characters or stories that have been done over and over again.

1. *Destry Rides Again* was a hit movie of the 1930s, but it had a life before and after that. Of the following actors, which one never played the part of Destry?

   a. Tom Mix   b. James Stewart   c. Audie Murphy
   d. Randolph Scott   e. Andy Griffith   f. John Gavin

2. Which of the following actors never played the Lone Ranger?

   a. Clayton Moore   b. John Hart
   c. Klinton Spilsbury   d. Charlton Heston

3. Matt Dillon was played by two different men, one on radio, and one on television. Which of the following was not one of those two?

   a. Ward Bond   b. James Arness   c. William Conrad

4. Wyatt Earp has been played by many actors. Which of the following never played him?

   a. James Garner   b. Henry Fonda   c. Hugh O'Brian
   d. Harris Yulin   e. Burt Lancaster   f. Gary Cooper

5. Wild Bill Hickok has also been played by many actors. Which of the following never played him?

   a. Gary Cooper   b. Guy Madison   c. Josh Brolin
   d. Tyrone Power

6. Two men have played Shane, one in the movies, and one on a short-lived TV series. Which of the following did not play Shane?

   a. Jack Palance   b. Alan Ladd   c. David Carradine

7. Scads of people have played Billy the Kid, either in the movies or on TV. Of the following, who hasn't?

   a. Paul Newman   b. Kris Kristofferson   c. Bob Dylan

d. Robert Taylor   e. Clu Gulager   f. Emilio Estevez
g. Michael J. Pollard

8. Gail Davis starred in the fifties TV series about her. Barbara
    Stanwyck played the title role in the movie about her. She was
    a sharpshooter with Buffalo Bill's Wild West Show. Name this
    legendary woman. _____

9. She's been portrayed in many TV westerns, and Doris Day
    played her in a 1953 movie that carried her name. She now lies
    buried next to Wild Bill Hickok in Deadwood, South Dakota.
    Name her. _____

10. Scott Forbes played him in the fifties series. Sterling Hayden and
    Richard Widmark have played him in the movies. He died at the
    Alamo, and his name remains famous because he designed a dis-
    tinctive bit of weaponry. Name him. _____

Test Number 5: **MUSIC ON THE TRAIL**

Though the real history of the American West isn't particularly musical,
the TV West has always been served up with musical accompaniment.
Can you answer these musical questions?

1. On what western would you have heard these words sung:
    "Rollin', rollin', rollin', keep those doggies rollin'"? _____

2. Who sang those words? _____

3. "The Ballad of Johnny Yuma" was the theme song for what
    western series? _____ Who sang it?

    _____

4. "Happy Trails to You" was _____'s theme song.

5. "The Ballad of Paladin" became a hit single. What show was it from? _____

6. According to its theme song, Wyatt Earp was "brave, _____ , and _____."

7. Fill in the blanks: "Davy, Davy Crockett, King of _____."

8. There's not much chance you know the answer to this question, but I'll bet you can hum the tune. The "Gunsmoke" theme is also known as _____ .

9. "Back in the Saddle Again" was _____ _____'s theme song.

10. He's the father of the star of "Three's Company," but he was a big singing cowboy in the thirties and forties, and his movies were a staple of fifties television. Can you name him? _____

Test Number 6: THINGS IN COMMON

In the following questions, all the people, places, or things have something in common. Can you pick out the patterns?

1. Merle Haggard, Ronald Reagan, Dale Robertson, Robert Taylor, and Stanley Andrews _____

2. Little Joe, Hoss, Ben, and Adam _____

3. Calling card, chess piece, mustache, and Hey Boy _____

4. Teaspoon, The Kid, Billy, and Jimmy _____

5. Bret, Bart, Ben, and Beauregard _____

6. Wishbone, Charlie Wooster, and Hop Sing _____

7. (Obscure question): "Elizabeth, My Love," "Inger, My Love," and "Marie, My Love" _____

8. Little Beaver (of "Red Ryder" fame), Baretta, and "Hardstep Rivers" _____

9. Robert Conrad as Pasquinel, Richard Chamberlain as Alexander McKeag, Michael Ansara as Lame Beaver, and Dennis Weaver as R. J. Poteet _____

10. Jarrod, Nick, Victoria, Audra, and Heath _____

Test Number 7:

OUR HEROES HAVE SOMETIMES BEEN COWBOYS

Match the TV hero to the actor who played him.

1. Bat Masterson _____   a. Ward Bond

2. Wyatt Earp _____   b. Robert Conrad

3. Cheyenne Bodie _____   c. Henry Fonda

4. Paladin _____   d. David Carradine

5. Josh Randall _____   e. Lee Horsley

6. Heath Barkley _____   f. Jock Mahoney

7. Ethan Allen Cord _____ g. Eric Fleming

8. Sugarfoot _____   h. Lorne Greene

9. Jim Redigo _____   i. Pat Conway

10. James T. West _____   j. Steve McQueen

11. Sheriff Clay Hollister _____ k. Hugh O'Brian

12. Marshal Simon Fry _____   l. Richard Boone

13. Shane _____   m. Clint Walker

14. Kwai Chang Caine _____ n. Richard Egan

15. Ben Cartwright _____   o. Robert Culp

16. Major Seth Adams _____ p. Will Hutchins

17. Gil Favor _____   q. Jay Silverheels

18. The Range Rider _____ r. Gene Barry

19. Hoby Gilman _____   s. Lee Majors

20. Tonto _____

1. It was a spoof of westerns back in 1967. It was called "Rango," and it starred a comedian who had earlier been seen on "McHale's Navy." Can you name him? _____

2. In 1973, Bob Denver made a western spoof that was a lot like "Gilligan's Island." He played a character called Dusty. Can you recall the series title? _____

3. Mostly forgotten now, it ran for four years and starred John Smith, Robert Fuller, and Hoagy Carmichael. Its title was taken from the name of a town in Wyoming.

   _____

4. It starred Neville Brand and Peter Brown, and it took its name from a town in Texas. _____

5. Can you name the character who taught Kwai Chang Caine?

   _____

6. He knew "when to hold 'em and when to fold 'em," both in the song and in the made-for-TV movies that bore the title

   _____

7. Michael Ansara played Apache chief Cochise on a series that took its name from a movie and a book called _____.

8. The son of the guy who played Dr. Steven Kiley on "Marcus Welby, M.D." plays Wild Bill Hickok on "The Young Riders." Name him. _____

9. "Tales of Wells Fargo," "The Iron Horse," and "J .J. Starbuck." What do those three shows have in common? _____

10. Sam Elliott and Tom Selleck teamed up for a miniseries back in 1982. It was drawn from the work of Louis L'Amour and it's often replayed on TNT. Can you name that series? _____

Answers

Test Number 1: **ONCE UPON A TIME IN THE WEST**

1. Bounty hunter Josh Randall was played by **Steve McQueen.**

2. **Wayne Rogers** starred in a series called "Stagecoach."

3. A gambler named Bret was played by **James Garner.**

4. Audra Barkley was played by **Linda Evans.**

5. Hoby Gilman on "Trackdown" was played by **Robert Culp.**

6. A young **Burt Reynolds** was half-breed blacksmith Quint Asper.

7. **Roger Moore** played Cousin Beauregard Maverick.

8. **David Carradine** first came to general attention as Shane.

9. The role of Paladin? **Richard Boone**

10. Little Joe was, of course, **Michael Landon.**

Test Number 2: LAST NAMES

1. Dennis Weaver played Chester **Goode**, Milburn Stone played Doc **Adams**, and Ken Curtis played Festus **Haggen**.

2. Barbara Stanwyck was the matriarch of the **Barkley** family.

3. Ben, Hoss, Little Joe, and Adam were all members of the **Cartwright** family.

4. The trail boss on "Rawhide" was Gil **Favor**.

5. Lee Horsley played Ethan **Cord**.

6. Leif Erickson played Big John, the patriarch of the **Cannon** clan.

7. Scott Brady played Shotgun **Slade**.

8. Robert Conrad played James T. **West**.

9. Lucas and Mark's last name was **McCain**.

10. Stephen Baldwin plays young Billy **Cody** and Josh Brolin plays young Jimmy **Hickok**.

Test Number 3: SOMEWHERE IN THE WEST

1 Matt, Kitty, Doc, Chester, and Festus were all residents of **Dodge City, Kansas**.

2. Paladin was based in **San Francisco**.

3. The Ponderosa was in the **Sierra Nevada**.

4. Lonesome Dove was a border place. On one side of the border

was **Texas** and on the other side was **Mexico**.

5. "The Big Valley" was set in the **San Joaquin Valley** in **California**.

6. "The High Chaparral" was set in Arizona Territory, which became the state of **Arizona**.

7. The Pony Express connected **St. Joseph**, Missouri, with **Sacramento**, California.

8. It was "the town too tough to die," both in reality and in this fifties series entitled **"Tombstone Territory."**

9. The valley where borax was mined was **Death Valley**, California, which was the setting for "Death Valley Days."

10. "The Rifleman" and his son lived in **North Fork, New Mexico**.

Test Number 4:

WHO WAS THAT MASKED MAN, ANYWAY?

1. **(d) Randolph Scott** was the only actor in this group who never played Destry.

2. **(e) Charlton Heston** never played the Lone Ranger.

3. **(a) Ward Bond** never played Matt Dillon.

4. **(f) Gary Cooper** never played Wyatt Earp.

5. **(d) Tyrone Power** never played Wild Bill.

6. **(a) Jack Palance** never appeared as Shane.

7. **(c) Bob Dylan** never played Billy the Kid.

8. **Annie Oakley** was a sharpshooter with Buffalo Bill's Wild West Show.

9. **Calamity Jane** lies buried next to Wild Bill Hickok in Deadwood, South Dakota.

10. **Jim Bowie**, who designed the bowie knife, died at the Alamo.

Answers

Test Number 5: **MUSIC ON THE TRAIL**

1. "Rollin', rollin', rollin', keep those doggies rollin' ": **"Rawhide"**

2. **Frankie Laine** sang those words.

3. "The Ballad of Johnny Yuma" was the theme song for **"The Rebel,"** and **Johnnie Cash** sang it.

4. "Happy Trails to You" was **Roy Roger**'s theme song.

5. "The Ballad of Paladin" was from **"Have Gun Will Travel."**

6. Wyatt Earp was "brave, **courageous,** and **bold."**

7. "Davy, Davy Crockett, King of **the Wild Frontier."**

8. The "Gunsmoke" theme is also known as **"Old Trails."**

9. "Back in the Saddle Again" was **Gene Autry**'s theme song.

10. **Tex Ritter** was a big singing cowboy in the thirties and forties.

Answers

1. **All these fellows hosted "Death Valley Days."**

2. Little Joe, Hoss, Ben, and Adam were **all members of the Cartwright family.**

3. Calling card, chess piece, mustache, and Hey Boy **are all associated with "Have Gun Will Travel."**

4. Teaspoon, The Kid, Billy, and Jimmy **were all Young Riders.**

5. Bret, Bart, Ben, and Beauregard **were all members of the Maverick family.**

6. Wishbone, Charlie Wooster, and Hop Sing **were all cooks.**

7. "Elizabeth, My Love," "Inger, My Love," and "Marie, My Love" **were all episodes of "Bonanza" concerning Ben Cartwright's dead wives.**

8. Little Beaver, Baretta, and "Hardstep Rivers" **are all characters Robert Blake has played.**

9. Robert Conrad as Pasquinel, Richard Chamberlain as Alexander McKeag, Michael Ansara as Lame Beaver, and Dennis Weaver as R. J. Poteet **were all members of the cast of "Centennial," the 1978–79 miniseries.**

10. Jarrod, Nick, Victoria, Audra, and Heath **were all members of the Barkley family on "The Big Valley."**

OUR HEROES HAVE SOMETIMES BEEN COWBOYS

Answers

1. Bat Masterson: **(r) Gene Barry**

2. Wyatt Earp: **(k) Hugh O'Brian**

3. Cheyenne Bodie: **(m) Clint Walker**

4. Paladin: **(l) Richard Boone**

5. Josh Randall: **(j) Steve McQueen**

6. Heath Barkley: **(s) Lee Majors**

7. Ethan Allen Cord: **(e) Lee Horsley**

8. Sugarfoot: **(p) Will Hutchins**

9. Jim Redigo: **(n) Richard Egan**

10. James T. West: **(b) Robert Conrad**

11. Sheriff Clay Hollister: **(i) Pat Conway**

12. Marshal Simon Fry: **(c) Henry Fonda**

13. Shane: **(d) David Carradine**

14. Kwai Chang Caine: **(d) David Carradine**

15. Ben Cartwright: **(h) Lorne Greene**

16. Major Seth Adams: **(a) Ward Bond**

17. Gil Favor: **(g) Eric Fleming**

18. The Range Rider: **(f) Jock Mahoney**

19. Hoby Gilman: **(o) Robert Culp**

20. Tonto: **(q) Jay Silverheels**

Test Number 8: **WESTERN ROUNDUP**

1. **Tim Conway** played Rango.

2. Bob Denver played Dusty on **"Dusty's Trail."**

3. Starring John Smith, Robert Fuller, and Hoagy Carmichael, the show was called **"Laramie."**

4. Neville Brand and Peter Brown starred in **"Laredo."**

5. The character who taught Kwai Chang Caine was **Master Po**.

6. He knew "when to hold 'em and when to fold 'em," both in the song and in the made-for-TV movies which bore the title **"The Gambler."**

7. Michael Ansara played Apache chief Cochise on **"Broken Arrow."**

8. **Josh Brolin** plays Wild Bill Hickok on **"The Young Riders."**

9. **Dale Robertson starred in all three shows**.

10. Sam Elliott and Tom Selleck teamed up for **"The Shadow Riders."**

Before we ride off into the sunset (and on to the next chapter), you might want to take a minute to check your score. Since the golden age of westerns on TV goes back some thirty years, you're not expected to do so well on this test.

Answers

Scoring

70-90 Correct: You know the West inside out—TV's version of it, anyway.

40-69 Correct: A fair hand.

20-39 Correct: A young dude. You occasionally visit out West, but you wouldn't want to live there.

0-19 Correct: A definite tenderfoot.

8

Spaced

"Beam me up, Scotty, there's no intelligent life on this planet."

BUMPER STICKER

Science fiction has not been particularly well represented on television. Cowboys and cops have far outnumbered robots and Romulans. But, for those die-hard sci-fi fans, there is life beyond "Star Trek," though surely not as much as they would like. This little chapter is a probe for that sci-fi life.

Join us now for this journey into deep space. Can you venture to where so many video explorers have gone before?

1. On the series titled "V," what did V stand for?_____

2. Complete the following and you will have named a sci-fi show from the 1960s: "There is nothing wrong with your TV set.

144

We are controlling transmission . . . You are watching a drama that reaches from the inner mind to _____."

3. Col. Steve Austin was a cyborg. What's a cyborg? _____

4. "There is a fifth dimension beyond that which is known to man. It is a dimension as vast as space." What did the man who said these words call that dimension? _____

5. Who was that narrator?_____

6. On "Lost in Space," who was the stowaway who got everyone lost in the first place? _____

7. "Star Trek" begat "Star Trek: The New Generation." "Star Trek: The New Generation begat": _____.

8. Capt. Steve Burton is piloting the "Spindrift" when it crashes. If you can name where it crashed, you'll name the series._____

9. In what city did "Alien Nation" take place?_____

10. What did the aliens on that show call themselves? _____

11. Robert Hays starred in the TV version of "Starman." Who had his part in the movie of the same name? _____

12. Though he uses a variant spelling, a member of the "Enterprise" shares a last name with one of the great writers of nineteeth-century Russia. Which one? _____

13. Another crew member has the name Uhura. What does that name mean in Swahili? _____

14. Spock is a half-breed. What were his parents? _____

15. These two planets caused the "Enterprise" most of its troubles.
_____ and _____

16. A staple of fifties television, Flash Gordon was often pitted against Ming the _____.

17. With the help of his scientist friend, Dr. _____ , Flash fought Ming, who was from the planet_____.

18. Steve Holland played Flash on TV, but the guy who played him in the movies is better remembered. Do you remember the star of the 1930s Flash Gordons, so often rerun on early TV?

_____

19. Who played Buck Rogers in the series "Buck Rogers in the 25th Century"? _____

20. That actor had a very short-lived series in 1990. In it, he headed up an organization known as Earth Alert Research Tactical Headquarters, or EARTH.
Can you name the series? _____

21. Commander Adama, Captain Apollo, and Lieutenant Starbuck could all be found aboard _____.

22. Who played Commander Adama? _____

23. Count Baltar and the Cylons. Good guys or bad guys?

_____

24. Easy one: Where did Superman come from? _____

25. Gary Graham and Eric Pierpoint had the lead roles in the TV version of "Alien Nation." Who played those roles in the movie version? _____ and _____

26. It made news when one of the Tenctonians had a baby—and it was heavily hyped. Why? _____

27. What book provided the basic premise for the series "Lost in Space"? _____

28. What was the kid's name who played Will Robinson on that show? _____

29. Did you happen to catch this one? It featured Ta'ra, a gorgeous alien who was trying to save herself—and Earth—from a monster that took over the bodies of its victims.
Sound familiar? _____

30. Name the 1987 miniseries based on the James Michener book about the history of the U.S. space program. _____

31. "Moonbase Alpha" and all of space provided the setting for this flashy sci-fi show starring Martin Landau. _____

32. There was a syndicated series called "War of the Worlds" that ran from 1988 to 1990. Who wrote the book it was drawn from?
_____

33. Who produced the radio version that scared America witless back in the 1930s? _____

34. Where did the aliens come from in the H. G. Wells novel? _____

35. Who played Mike Donovan, the resistance leader on "V"?
_____

36. A once-famous real-life newscaster introduced most episodes of "V." Which newsman was that? _____

37. Answer this question, and you've named this mid-eighties series.
Dr. Billy Hayes organized "El" Lincoln, "Johnny B" Bukowski, and Gloria Dinallo into a unit called _____ .

38. Not sci-fi exactly, but it took a page from sci-fi's book: This show featured Ray Walston as Martin (get it?) O'Hara.
Name it. _____

39. We don't often take note of executive producers, but Trekkies know the name of the guy who produced their show.
Do you? _____

40. More supernatural than sci-fi, this series came after "The Twilight Zone" and was also introduced and hosted by Rod Serling.
Remember its title? _____

41. Complete the title of this late-fifties/early-sixties series:
"One Step _____."

42. It borrowed heavily from the success of *The Terminator*, and it featured a character named Jesse, an alien warrior who had been exiled to Earth because he was too violent back home. The name of the series was _____ .

43. Which two of the following *were not* members of either crew of the "Enterprise": Kirk, Scotty, Schultzy, Sulu, Bones, Spock, Crusher, Data, Krelnem, Yar, Worf. _____

44. Not sci-fi, but I wonder if you remember the astronaut played by Bill Dana on "The Steve Allen Show." _____

45. On "Saturday Night Live," the Coneheads are from the planet _____ but they claim to be from _____ .

46. Mork's native tongue? _____

47. The movie *Star Trek II* was developed from an episode on "Star Trek" called "Space Seed." The actor who played Khan starred in both the movie and that episode.
Name him. _____

48. She plays Guinan, the bartender on "The Next Generation."
_____

49. You only lived to age thirty in "The City of Domes," so this guy took off just before his birthday. Gregory Harrison played him in the short-lived series, which had been a movie before that. Name the movie and the series. _____

50. In 1967–68, actor Roy Thinnes played a guy who believed that alien invaders were in our midst. He had a hard time convincing anyone. Do you remember the name of the series, or have aliens taken control of your brain? _____

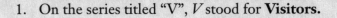

Chapter 8: SPACED

Answers

1. On the series titled "V", *V* stood for **Visitors.**

2. "There is nothing wrong with your TV set. We are controlling transmission . . . You are watching a drama that reaches from the inner mind to **"The Outer Limits."**

3. A cyborg is **part human/part machine**.

4. "There is a fifth dimension beyond that which is known to man. It is a dimension as vast as space." It's called **"The Twilight Zone."**

5. The narrator of "The Twilight Zone" was **Rod Serling**.

6. The stowaway who got everyone lost in the first place was **Jonathan Harris as Dr. Zachary Smith.**

7. "Star Trek" begat "Star Trek: The New Generation." "Star Trek: The New Generation" begat **Deep Space Nine**.

8. The "Spindrift" crashed in the **Land of the Giants**.

9. "Alien Nation" took place in **Los Angeles.**

10. Those aliens called themselves **Newcomers**.

11. **Jeff Bridges** starred in the movie version of *Starman*.

12. **Ensign Chekov** shares a last name with the nineteenth-century Russian writer **Anton Chekhov.**

13. Uhura means **Freedom**.

14. Spock's **father was a Vulcan; his mother was an earthling**.

15. The two alien races that caused the "Enterprise" most of its troubles were **Romulans** and **Klingons.**

16. Flash Gordon was often pitted against Ming the **Merciless.**

17. With the help of Dr. **Zharkov,** Flash fought Ming, who was from the planet **Mongo.**

18. **Buster Crabbe** was the star of the 1930s Flash Gordon pictures and serials.

19. **Gil Gerard** played Buck Rogers in the series "Buck Rogers in the 25th Century."

20. Gil Gerard had a short-lived series in 1990 called **"E.A.R.T.H. Force."**

21. Commander Adama, Captain Apollo, and Lieutenant Starbuck could all be found aboard the **Battlestar Galactica.**

22. **Lorne Greene** played Commander Adama.

23. Count Baltar and the Cylons were **bad.**

24. Superman come from **Krypton.**

25. **James Caan** and **Mandy Patinkin** had the lead roles in the movie *Alien Nation.*

26. The Tenctonian baby **had a father for a mother—the father gave birth.**

27. *The Swiss Family Robinson* was the book that provided the basic premise for the series "Lost in Space."

28. **Bill Mumy** played Will Robinson.

29. Ta'ra, a gorgeous alien, was trying to save herself—and Earth—on **"Something Is Out There."** (It ran two months in 1988.)

30. The name of the 1987 miniseries based on the James Michener book about the history of the U.S. space program was **"Space."**

31. "Moonbase Alpha" was the setting for **"Space: 1999."**

32. **H. G. Wells** wrote the book that "War of the Worlds" was drawn from.

33. **Orson Welles** produced the radio version that scared America witless.

34. The aliens in the Wells novel came from **Mars**.

35. Mike Donovan was played by **Marc Singer**.

36. **Howard K. Smith** introduced most episodes of "V."

37. Dr. Billy Hayes organized "El" Lincoln, "Johnny B" Bukowski, and Gloria Dinallo into a unit called **"Misfits of Science."**

38. Ray Walston played Martin O'Hara in **"My Favorite Martian."**

39. Trekkies know **Gene Roddenberry**'s name.

40. **"Night Gallery"** was more supernatural than sci-fi.

41. "One Step **Beyond.**"

42. The name of the series that borrowed heavily from *The Terminator* was **"Hard Time on Planet Earth."**

43. **Schultzy** and **Krelnem** were not members of either of the "Enterprise" crews.

44. The astronaut played by Bill Dana was **Jose Jimenez.**

45. The Coneheads are from the planet **Remulak**, but they claim to be from **France.**

46. Mork's native tongue was **Orkan.**

47. The actor who played Khan was **Ricardo Montalban.**

48. **Whoopi Goldberg** plays Guinan, the bartender on "The Next Generation."

49. The movie and the series are called **"Logan's Run."**

50. Actor Roy Thinnes played in the series **"The Invaders."**

Answers

That little test should give you an idea of just how spacey you are. If I failed to ask about your favorite character or show, then you watch more sci-fi than I do. Check the answers. A score of over 30 would suggest that you've done warp time in front of the tube.

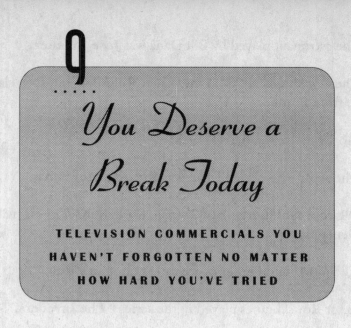

9

You Deserve a Break Today

**TELEVISION COMMERCIALS YOU
HAVEN'T FORGOTTEN NO MATTER
HOW HARD YOU'VE TRIED**

"You can tell the ideals of a nation by its advertisements."
NORMAN DOUGLAS

*"What is most disconcerting is that by age eleven . . .
most children have become cynical—ready to
believe that, like advertising, business and other
institutions are riddled with hypocrisy."*
HARVARD BUSINESS REVIEW

This chapter is constructed to test your memory of commercials, jingles, songs, tag lines, images, and no-longer-advertised products that imprinted themselves on our individual and collective memories.

They don't kid around about this stuff. More money is spent on a minute of advertising time than on any comparable minute of broadcasting. All the creative energies Madison Avenue can muster are directed to contriving words and images that last, that stay with you, that you won't be able to forget. Have you been able to forget them? I bet not.

Some of them have been around for a very long time, predating television by decades. Did you know that Prudential Insurance's phrase "the strength of Gibraltar" dates back to 1896? That slogan is the ancestor of one Prudential uses today, a slogan you know well and will find in the tests below.

The phrase "Breakfast of Champions" was first used in 1922 to promote a cereal I'll bet you can name. (Wheaties)

"The Beer That Made Milwaukee Famous" goes all the way back to the nineteenth century. What beer is that, anyway? (Schlitz)

And you surely know what product is associated with the phrase "When it rains, it pours." That goes all the way back to 1911. Do you know the product? (Morton Salt)

"Good to the last drop" goes back even further, to 1907, and I'm sure you know *what* is good to the last drop. You know it's coffee, and you probably know what brand. (Maxwell House)

Advertising has also given us words or phrases that didn't exist until some ad agency dreamt them up and repeated them endlessly on television. Madison Avenue gave us "waxy yellow buildup" in the 1950s, "antiperspirant" in the 1960s, and "jock itch" in the 1970s. Whether we needed them or not, I'll leave up to you. Even the phrase "television commercial" is recent; it first gained currency in the 1940s, and it hasn't been out of our vocabularies since. And the phrase "TV dinner" was first heard in the early 1950s, a name trademarked by Swanson, a frozen-food company made famous by advertising.

So, try your hand at this test of commercials. Like it or not, memories are made of this stuff, too.

Test Number 1: SLOGANEERING

Let your memory be the adman or adwoman. Fill in the blanks to complete the following famous commercials.

1. "Nothin' says lovin' like_____
   _____ , and _____ says it best."

2. "Don't just _____ it out, _____ it out."

3. "I've fallen, and I _____."

4. "You got the right one, baby, _____."

5. "_____: Don't leave home _____."

6. "Get a piece of the _____."

7. "Fly the _____ of _____."

8. "With a name like _____ , it's got to be_____."

9. "Good to the last _____."

10. "You're in good _____ with _____."

11. "I'm a _____ , she's a _____ , wouldn't you like to be a _____ , too?"

12. "Aren't you glad you use _____ , don't you wish _____?"

13. "_____, the San Francisco Treat."

14. "It takes a licking and keeps on _____."

15. "It doesn't get any better than _____."

16. "Ace is the place with the _____."

17. "I want my _____."

18. "Try it—you'll _____."

19. "See the U.S.A. in your _____ ."

20. "Pardon me, but do you have any _____ ?"

21. "Mama mia, that's a _____ ."

22. "GE: We bring _____ ."

23. "My bologna has a first name—it's _____ ."

24. "Oh, I wish I were an _____ ."

25. "I'd like to teach the world to _____

In perfect _____

I'd like to buy the world a _____

And keep it _____ ;

It's the _____ . . ."

Test Number 2: SPOKESPERSONS

Advertising borrows many of its techniques from the world of propaganda. One of the most commonly used propaganda techniques is called a "testimonial." The idea behind this technique is that people will associate an idea, a political party, or a product with the favorable attributes and virtues of loved or respected celebrities. So it is that advertisers will pay huge sums of money to have popular people associate themselves with their products. And it tends to work. As a nation, we love Bill Cosby and, as the theory goes, we transfer some of that love to the products he endorses.

If it didn't work, if it didn't succeed in pouring lots of money into corporate coffers, it's doubtful that companies would pay the extraordinary sums they pay to celebrity spokespersons. Did you know, for instance, that the fee paid to Michael Jordan for endorsing Nike products would pay the salary of one of Nike's Indonesian workers for nearly forty-five thousand years.

I'll bet you do very well on this next test—which will demonstrate just how well the technique works.

CELEBRITY SPOKESPERSONS

Match the celebrities below with the products they've endorsed.

26. Anita Bryant _____   a.   Maytag

27. Ricardo Montalban _____   b.   Serta

28. Charlton Heston _____   c.   Hertz

29. James Garner/
    Mariette Hartley _____   d.   Thighmaster

                              e.   Chrysler
30. Candice Bergen _____

                              f.   Florida orange juice
31. Martha Raye _____

                              g.   National Rifle
32. Jessie White/
    Gordon Jump _____   Association

33. Joey Heatherton _____   h.   Polaroid Land Camera

34. Suzanne Somers _____   i.   Sprint

35. O. J. Simpson _____   j.   Polident

36. Bill Cosby _____   k.   Fantastik

37. Karl Malden _____	l. Kentucky Fried Chicken
38. Ray Charles _____	m. Player's Club
39. Victor Kiam _____	n. Budweiser
40. Telly Savalas _____	o. Remington
41. June Allyson _____	p. Chevrolet
42. Ed McMahon _____	q. Pepsi
43. Janine Turner _____	r. American Express
44. M. C. Hammer _____	s. Depends
45. Elayne Boosler _____	t. Jell-O
46. Joan Lunden _____	u. Tylenol
47. Angela Lansbury _____	v. Vaseline Intensive Care
48. Doc Severinsen _____	w. Equal
49. Richard Petty _____	x. Bugles Corn Shells
50. Cher _____	y. STP

FICTIONAL SPOKESPERSONS

If the ad agency doesn't want to spend the money required to purchase
the services of a real flesh-and-blood celebrity, they can make up its
own. Match the following fictional representatives with the products

they were created to represent.

51. Tony the Tiger _____   a. Xerox

52. Speedy _____   b. Charmin

53. Poppin' Fresh _____   c. Folgers

54. Morris the Cat _____   d. Alka-Seltzer

55. Charlie the Tuna _____   e. Comet

56. Josephine,
    the Lady Plumber _____   f. 9-Lives

57. Mr. Whipple _____   g. Starkist

58. Mrs. Olsen _____   h. Pillsbury

59. Madge, the manicurist _____   i. Kellogg's

60. Brother Dominic _____   j. Colgate-Palmolive

Test Number 3: **PRODUCT IDENTIFICATION**

The lines of ad copy in the following test are all well remembered, if for no other reason than the fact that we heard them so often. But did they work? Do you know the product being promoted in the following lines?

61. "It keeps going, and going, and going." What keeps "going, and going, and going"? _____

62. It "took a licking, and kept on ticking." What took a licking?

_____

63. Who wanted you to "reach out and touch someone"?

_____

64. Who got us all worried about "ring around the collar"?

_____

65. "I can't believe I ate the whole thing," he said, before reaching for this product. What product? _____

66. According to this eatery, "you deserve a break today." Who thought you deserved a break? _____

67. This sexy model urged us to "take it off, take it *all* off." What product was she selling? _____

68. Edie Adams sang, "Hey big spender, spend a little dime on me." What product was she pitching? _____

69. The line went: "If you've got the time, we've got the beer." What kind of beer? _____

70. Fill in the blank: "Leggo my _____."

71. "Is it true blondes have more fun?" That was the line. What was the product? _____

72. "Let's get Mikey. He won't eat it. He hates everything." That was what one little boy said about his brother in this commercial for _____ . (It turned out, of course, that Mikey liked it.)

73. "We do it all for you" was what they told us back in the seventies. Who did it all for us?_____

74. Charles Schultz's "Peanuts" characters were used to sell us insurance using the slogan "Get _____ ." Get what?

75. Bart Simpson pitches a candy bar. Which one?_____

76. It put "a tiger in your tank." What did?_____

77. Complete the following: " _____ , the foaming cleanser, floats the dirt right down the drain."

78. She said, "I like my men in _____ , or nothing at all." Fill in the blank and you will have named the product.

79. "When you care enough to send the very best" was a long-used slogan. For whom?_____

80. It was "stronger than dirt." What was?_____

81. "Try it, you'll like it" was the key phrase in a series of ads in the 1970s for_____ .

82. This product pitched itself to "regular people, who sometimes aren't." Name the product._____

83. "Can't beat the real thing." According to this ad, what's the "real thing"? _____

84. "It's two, two, two mints in one." What is?_____

85. "Give your breath long-lasting freshness with _____ ."

86. "Moistens your mouth . . . and freshens your breath while you chew." What does? _____

87. When we "Ask Dr. Mom," what does she tell us?_____

88. It promised us "the comfort shave."_____

89. "My doctor said _____."

90. "Step into a man's world. Step into a world with action. In a man's world, you know when you've done your best. Step into a man's world with _____ ."

91. "For a treat instead of a treatment, treat yourself to _____ .

92. "Look sharp. Feel sharp. Be sharp," with _____.

93. "Won't fill you up. Won't let you down. You get a smile every time with a _____."

94. "_____ , with the Micronite filter, smoked by more scientists, more educators than any other cigarette."

95. "Be happy, go _____."

96. "Stay on the beam—eat energy-packed _____ ."

97. "We will sell no wine before its time." _____

98. "Come alive. You're in the _____ generation."

99. "Betcha can't eat just one." _____

100. "You can count on us." _____

101. "We put you in the driver's seat."_____

You Deserve a Break Today

102. "I don't wanna grow up, I'm a _____ kid."

103. "A sprinkle a day helps keep odor away." _____

104. "I feel like chicken tonight." _____

105. "Sometimes you feel like a nut; sometimes you don't."
     What product? _____

1. "Nothin' says lovin' like **something from the oven** and **Pillsbury** says it best."

2. "Don't just **wash** it out, **Shout** it out."

3. "I've fallen, and I **can't get up**."

4. "You got the right one, baby, **uh-huh**."

5. "**American Express**: Don't leave home **without it**."

6. "Get a piece of the **rock**."

7. "Fly the **friendly skies** of **United**."

8. "With a name like **Smucker's**, it's got to be **good**."

9. "Good to the last **drop**."

10. "You're in good **hands** with **Allstate**."

11. "I'm a **Pepper**, she's a **Pepper**, wouldn't you like to be a **Pepper**, too?"

12. "Aren't you glad you use **Dial**; don't you wish **everybody did**?"

13. "**Rice-A-Roni**, the San Francisco Treat."

14. "It takes a licking and keeps on **ticking**."

15. "It doesn't get any better than **this**."

16. "Ace is the place with the **helpful hardware man**."

Answers

17. "I want my **Maypo**."

18. "Try it—you'll **like it**."

19. "See the U.S.A. in your **Chevrolet**."

20. "Pardon me, but do you have any **Grey Poupon**?"

21. "Mama mia, that's a **spicy meatball**."

22. "G.E.: We bring **bring good things to life**."

23. "My bologna has a first name—it's **O-s-c-a-r**."

24. "Oh, I wish I were an **Oscar Mayer wiener**."

25. "I'd like to teach the world to **sing**
    In perfect **harmony**;
    I'd like to buy the world a **Coke**
    And keep it **company**;
    It's the **real thing** . . ."

Test Number 2: CELEBRITY SPOKESPERSONS

26. Anita Bryant: **(f) Florida orange juice**

27. Ricardo Montalban: **(e) Chrysler**

28. Charlton Heston: **(g) National Rifle Association**

29. James Garner/Mariette Hartley: **(h) Polaroid Land Camera**

30. Candice Bergen: **(i) Sprint**

31. Martha Raye: **(j) Polident**

32. Jessie White/Gordon Jump: **(a) Maytag**

33. Joey Heatherton: **(b) Serta**

34. Suzanne Somers: **(d) Thighmaster**

35. O. J. Simpson: **(c) Hertz**

36. Bill Cosby: **(t) Jell-O**

37. Karl Malden: **(r) American Express**

38. Ray Charles: **(q) Pepsi**

39. Victor Kiam: **(o) Remington**

40. Telly Savalas: **(m) Player's Club**

41. June Allyson: **(s) Depends**

42. Ed McMahon: **(n) Budweiser**

43. Janine Turner: **(p) Chevrolet**

44. M. C. Hammer: **(l) Kentucky Fried Chicken**

45. Elayne Boosler: **(k) Fantastik**

46. Joan Lunden: **(v) Vaseline Intensive Care**

47. Angela Lansbury: **(u) Tylenol**

48. Doc Severinsen: **(x) Bugles Corn Shells**

You Deserve a Break Today

49. Richard Petty: **(y) STP**

50. Cher: **(w) Equal**

Answers

FICTIONAL SPOKESPERSONS

51. Tony the Tiger: **(i) Kellogg's**

52. Speedy: **(d) Alka-Seltzer**

53. Poppin' Fresh: **(h) Pillsbury**

54. Morris the Cat: **(f) 9-Lives**

55. Charlie the Tuna: **(g) Starkist**

56. Josephine, the lady plumber: **(e) Comet**

57. Mr. Whipple: **(b) Charmin**

58. Mrs. Olsen: **(c) Folgers**

59. Madge, the manicurist: **(j) Colgate-Palmolive**

60. Brother Dominic: **(a) Xerox**

Test Number 3: **PRODUCT IDENTIFICATION**

61. **Energizer batteries** apparently go on forever.

62. **Timex watches** seemed to tick forever.

63. **AT&T** called on us to reach out and touch someone.

64. The scourge of ring around the collar could be wiped out with **Wisk**.

65. If you ate the whole thing you needed **Alka-Seltzer**.

66. **McDonald's** thought we deserved a break.

67. The sexy model was selling **Noxema shaving cream**.

68. Edie Adams was the **Muriel cigar** lady.

69. **Miller** was the beer, if we had the time.

70. "Leggo my **Eggo**."

71. **Clairol** would have had us believe that blondes have more fun.

72. Mikey liked **Life cereal.**

73. Not only did it give us a break, **McDonald's** did everything else for us, too.

74. The "Peanuts" gang wanted us to "Get **Met**"—**Metropolitan Life Insurance.**

75. Bart likes **Butterfingers**.

76. **Exxon gasoline** put a tiger in your tank.

77. **Ajax** was the foaming cleanser.

78. She wanted her men in **English Leather**, cologne and after-shave.

79. **Hallmark** was what we sent "when we cared enough to send the very best."

80. **Ajax** was "stronger than dirt."

81. We tried it; it didn't agree with us, so we needed **Alka-Seltzer**.

82. **Ex-Lax** was for "regular people, who sometimes aren't."

83. **Coke** is the "real thing."

84. **Certs** claims to be two mints in one.

85. **Big Red chewing gum** gives your breath "long-lasting freshness."

86. **Dentyne** "moistens your mouth . . . and freshens your breath while you chew."

87. Dr. Mom recommends **Robitussin cough medicine.**

88. **Norelco** promised us "the comfort shave."

89. "My doctor said **Mylanta**."

90. "Step into a man's world with **Vaseline hair tonic**."

91. "For a treat instead of a treatment, treat yourself to **Old Gold** cigarettes."

92. "Look sharp. Feel sharp. Be sharp," with **Gillette razor blades.**

93. "Won't fill you up. Won't let you down. You get a smile every time with a **Ballantine beer.**"

94. Back in the 1950s, **Kent cigarettes** had the Micronite filter. Whether it was really smoked by more scientists and educators is a matter for speculation.

95. "Be happy, go **Lucky**," with Lucky Strike cigarettes.

96. "Stay on the beam—eat energy-packed **Sunbeam bread**."

97. According to Orson Welles, and others, **Paul Masson** would "sell no wine before its time."

98. "Come alive. You're in the **Pepsi** generation."

99. You couldn't eat just one **Lay's potato chip**.

100. **Sears** assures us: "You can count on us."

101. **Hertz** promised to "put you in the driver's seat."

102. "I don't wanna grow up, I'm a **Toys "R" Us** kid."

103. "A sprinkle a day helps keep odor away." **Shower to Shower deodorant powder**.

104. "I feel like chicken tonight." Presumably, because of **Ragu** sauces.

105. "Sometimes you feel like a nut: sometimes you don't" was the slogan for **Peter Paul Almond Joy and Mounds candy bars**.

Answers

However you might have scored on this test, you'll probably wish you'd scored lower. These slogans are like mind clutter, and it's nearly impossible to clean this particular attic. However well you did on the test, advertisers are going to wish you'd done better. Since I'm not an advertiser (and presumably, neither are you), I'm going to score this test in reverse order. The more you missed, the better off you are.

Scoring

75–105 Incorrect: Your mind is relatively uncluttered.

45–74 Incorrect: They got through to you, no matter how quick you were with the remote.

0–44 Incorrect: No wonder you can't remember your anniversary. And this explains all that stuff you own that you never use.

10

Soaped Up

> *"Hope, finally, is what the soap opera is all about;*
> *the usually illusory hope that maybe, just perhaps,*
> *tomorrow will deal a new hand."*
>
> RUTH ROSEN

There's always a crisis on the soaps. People tend to be very attractive on the soaps. Long-lost relatives are always turning up. People frequently learn that they are related to people they didn't know were kin. There are lots of twins on the soaps. Quite often, one twin is good and the other twin is evil. People on the soaps frequently get sick, and they tend to have rather exotic diseases. Perhaps—though this cannot be certified—there is more scheming, conniving, back-stabbing, betrayal, lying, cheating, and stealing in soap land than in real life. Surely there are a great many unwed mothers, though the percentage of bastards born on television is probably even lower than in real life, especially if we count the metaphorical bastards we tend to meet. There's a good deal of amnesia on the soaps; characters are afflicted with this disease whenever the writers need a bit of forgetfulness as a plot contrivance.

Another kind of amnesia sometimes afflicts those viewers who try to remember all those plots, all those characters, all those soaps that have come and gone over the years. This chapter will test whether you suffer that affliction. If you watch the soaps, how much do you remember? If you don't watch soaps, how much of this cultural information has filtered through to you anyway?

You can't talk or think about television without taking soap operas into consideration. Soaps have been a part of television since its inception. For commercial television, soap operas have been a gold mine, routinely accounting for a major share of the networks' profits. Loyal viewers, low production costs, and dependable advertisers like Procter & Gamble have made soap operas a television staple throughout its history. And it's not just daytime TV anymore; soaps have long since established a solid beachhead in prime time with popular shows like "Dynasty" and "Dallas," along with a host of clones.

Soaps predate television, of course. They were an essential element of radio, too, weaving stories over generations and featuring broad ranges of characters.

I'll admit that I've never been a soap opera viewer. In that area, as in some others, my credentials are unimpressive. I suspect that there are two primary reasons why I've never gotten hooked on soaps: 1. I'm male, and 2. I'm something of a snob. Women have always formed the larger percentage of soap opera viewers, and soaps have long been an easy thing for snobs to sneer at. In a survey taken in 1980, women accounted for 79 percent of the soap opera audience, men for 21 percent. The percentage of snobs who watch soaps is unavailable; a real snob would never admit to watching them.

Since 1980, however, male viewership has increased as lifestyles have changed. Great numbers of male college students, for instance, are hooked on one or another of the popular daytime soap operas. Each day, more than eleven hours of daytime soap opera programming is broadcast for those students to watch. If they are average, they will watch about nine hours of it each week. Surely there's nothing effeminate about watching soap operas. If you need a macho role model to salve any male insecurities you may harbor about watching soaps, you might appreciate knowing that NBA great Charles Barkley (certainly no wimp) was once late for a game because he couldn't tear himself away from an episode of "All My Children."

Even if you don't watch soaps, you might be surprised at how much you've picked up about them. If TV is a major purveyor and expression of our culture, then a good bit of that culture is reflected in the soaps, even if measured only by the amount of broadcasting time it consumes. But its influence goes beyond the box; it's there all the time—in the conversations of friends, in the checkout lines at the supermarket, and on the entertainment shows that tell us all about people unknown to us, and shows we may never have watched. Even if you've never seen "All My Children," you've surely heard of it, and you've probably heard of Susan Lucci, too. (She's the one who's been nominated for scads of Emmys, but has long been denied that prize.)

So, see how much you know, or don't know, about the shadowland of soap operas, these parallel universes and megalives that hold such a grip on the American imagination.

Test Number 1: 99 & 44/100ths% FAMILIAR

Soap opera addicts know the programs by their initials. *Soap Opera Digest* and other publications routinely abbreviate the names of the shows. If you know your soaps, you'll know what these initials represent.

1. AMC is _____

2. OLTL is _____

3. GH is _____

4. Y&R is _____

5. AW is _____

6. ATWT is _____

7. B&B is _____

8. SB is _____

9. FC is _____

10. GL is _____

Test Number 2: **SOAP SATIRE**

Some people might say that the soap opera form satirizes itself, but there have been plenty of satires written and performed about soap operas. The conventions of soap operas are easy enough to satirize. Do you know the answer to these questions about movies or television that made fun of the soaps?

1. What was the name of the soap opera satire Johnny Carson used to do regularly on "The Tonight Show"?

    _____

2. It was a movie, but maybe you caught it on HBO. What was the name of the soap opera send-up that starred Sally Field and Kevin Kline?_____

3. What was the name of the satirical series in which Billy Crystal played a homosexual?

    _____

4. "The Carol Burnett Show" used to have a running skit about a soap opera. What was the name of that show within a show?

_____

5. One of Mary Hartman's main worries had to do with her kitchen floor. What was she worried about?

_____

6. A 1986 miniseries that satirized soaps, it starred Carol Burnett and Dabney Coleman, and was set in an agricultural town in California. Name that town and you've named this soap satire.

_____

7. A character from the satirical series "Soap" spun off into his own series. That character was played by Robert Guillaume. The series was named after his character. Name that spin-off.

_____

8. "Mary Hartman, Mary Hartman," a satire of soap operas, spun off a satire of talk shows. Name that spin-off.

_____

9. It satirized soap opera conventions in the darkest of tones, and it was created by David Lynch. Set in the Pacific Northwest, it attracted enormous attention in the early 1990s. Name it.

_____

10. Name the two principal families on "Soap."

_____

Test Number 3: SOAP FLAKES

Some general questions about soap operas.

1. The longest running-soap opera on television is_____ .

2. She played Joanne Gardner Barron Tate Vincente Tourneur, thrice widowed and four times married over her thirty-five years on the show. Name the show. _____
    Name the actress who played her all those years. _____

3. The cast of a popular soap made a TV movie called *The Cradle Will Fall* in 1983. What soap opera cast made this migration to prime time?_____

4. The largest audience ever to watch a soap occurred when Luke and Laura were married in 1981.
    Name the soap. _____

5. Easy one. Complete the following phrase: "Like sands through an hourglass, so _____ ."

6. This ex-wife of a New York real estate tycoon played herself on "One Life to Live." Who's herself?_____

7. The woman who stole the tycoon away from the aforementioned divorcée did a stint on "Loving."
    Name the "other woman." _____

8. And, to complete the set, the Man himself turned up in a scene with Susan Lucci on "All My Children." If you knew the other two, then you know him. _____

9. It was the first daytime soap to win an Emmy (in 1972), but that didn't save it from cancellation ten years later. It concerned

events in and around Hope Memorial Hospital, and it was called

_____ .

10. It was the first daytime soap in which one of the major families was black, but it lasted less than two seasons, from 1989 to 1991. Can you name it?_____

11. What's the title of the "soap within a soap" on "One Life To Live"?_____

12. In the world of soaps, what did Dr. Joyce Brothers and Sammy Davis, Jr. have in common?_____

13. Before he was Grant Harrison on "All My Children," he was Jack Ewing on "Dallas." Before that, he starred with Walter Brennan in a western series called "The Guns of Will Sonnett." Do you know his name?_____

14. Viewers decided the verdict in Brittany Peterson's trial for attempted murder on this show. What show?_____

15. Writers don't get much recognition, but if you're a soap fan, you probably know the name of the veteran soap writer who created "All My Children."_____

16. Though relatively rare in real life, this disease has always been quite common among soap opera characters. Can you remember the name of the disease, or have you lost your memory?

_____

17. Despite her popularity, and after thirteen nominations, she still has not won an Emmy._____

18. The first legal abortion in soap history: Name the character who had it. _____

19. She's now Kelly Bundy, but she first appeared as a babe in her real mother's arms on "Days of Our Lives." _____

20. Soap writers seem to like these dual roles (two actors for the price of one, I guess). He plays Adam and Stuart Chandler on "All My Children," but he was once Candy on "Bonanza." _____

21. First she was Mrs. Johnson, then she appeared more regularly as Verla Grubbs. Her roles were created for her because she was a fan. Name the actress, and the soap. _____

22. The granddaughter of Robert Mitchum and the son of John Wayne both appear in this soap. She plays Donna Logan; he plays Storm Logan. (Storm? Is that a soap opera name, or what?) Name the soap. _____

23. The theme song from "The Young and the Restless" has an Olympic connection.
Can you name the song?_____

24. As far as I know, he's the only son of a U.S. president to appear regularly on a soap. He played Andy Richards on "The Young and the Restless." Who's his daddy?_____

25. Unless you're of a certain age, you won't remember this soap. It had a twenty-one-year run on radio, and a five-year run on television, from 1958–1963. It was called "Young Dr. _____ ."

26. His name is Avery Schreiber. He plays Leopold Von Leuschner on "Days of Our Lives," but he was once half the comedy team of _____ and Schreiber.

27. Her real name is Edna Rae Gilhooley. She won an Oscar for her work in the Martin Scorsese film *Alice Doesn't Live Here Anymore*. In the mid-sixties, she was Dr. Kate Bartok on "The Doctors." Do you know her stage name?_____

28. She went on to "Charlie's Angels" and "Scarecrow and Mrs. King," but she once played Daphne Harridge on "Dark Shadows." _____

29. She's the only real Dame to have appeared as a regular on a soap. She won an Emmy as Lady Macbeth, but much wider exposure for her villainy as Minx Lockridge. Name her, and the soap.

   _____

30. What do the following things have in common: Rodi's Tavern, St. James Church, Giorgio's, the Banner, Wanda's Place, Serenity Springs, and WVLE Radio? _____

31. What do the following things have in common: Happy Homes Bungalows, Cedars Hospital, Spaulding Enterprises, Wheels and Meals, Lewis Oil, and The Regency Hotel?

   _____

32. If you follow the traumas and trials of Lee Ann and Jason, Andrew, Billy, Suede, Luna, Max, Clint, and Sloan, then you're a regular watcher of "_____."

33. If you know all about Clay, Leo, Ava, Christopher, Trisha, Giff, and the McKenzies, then you're hooked on "_____."

34. If Jenna, Alex, Alan-Michael, Harley, Mallet, Blake, and Ross are part of your life, then you've been watching "_____."

35. Erica, Brian, Dixie, Livia, Lucas, Terence, Taylor, Galen, Carter, and Nurse Marsh are all to be found on "_____."

36. Which of the following *are not* characters on "The Bold and the Beautiful"? a. Brooke b. Macy c. Elmer d. Spectra e. Ridge f. Casanova g. the Marquis de Sade_____

37. In 1981, this soap opera couple made the cover of *Newsweek*.

Elizabeth Taylor was in attendance at their fictional wedding. Name the show, and name the couple. _____

38. Where would you go to find the following places: PVU, the Chateau, the Goal Post, Wildwind, and Cortland Manor?

_____

39. Rory Calhoun, former cowboy star of the 1950s, starred as Judge Judson Tyler on this now-defunct soap set in Washington, D.C. Do you remember the name of this one?_____

40. "Ryan's Hope": What was the series named for?_____

Test Number 4: **SOAP SITES**

Match the location to the soap opera.

1. Henderson _____   a. "Brighter Day"

2. Springfield _____   b. "Loving"

3. Pine Valley _____   c. "Love of Life"

4. Genoa City _____   d. "Secret Storm"

5. Los Angeles _____   e. "Guiding Light"

6. Port Charles _____   f. "As the World Turns"

7. Chicago _____   g. "One Life to Live"

8. Barrowsville/Rosehill _____   h. "Days of Our Lives"

9. Corinth _____   i. "One Man's Family"

10. Collingsport _____   j. "The Edge of Night"

11. Salem _____   k. "The Bold and the
                                            Beautiful"

12. Llanview _____   l. "Another World"

13. Bay City _____   m. "Soap"

14. Monticello _____   n. "The Young and the
                                            Restless"

15. Santa Barbara _____
                                         o. "Mary Hartman, Mary
16. Oakdale _____   Hartman"

                                         p. "Dark Shadows"

17. Fernwood _____   q. "Search for Tomorrow"

18. Denver _____   r. "Dynasty"

19. New Hope _____   s. "Generations"

20. Woodbridge _____   t. "General Hospital"

21. Dunn's River _____   u. "Santa Barbara"

22. San Francisco _____   v. "All My Children"

Test Number 5: **SOAP BUBBLES**

They Made It Big

It's sometimes surprising to find that many of our major movie and television stars once worked rather unnoticed in daytime television. In the test that follows, you may or may not be surprised to find that you know or don't know the early work of some of these major film figures.

1. She went on to major acclaim, including her Oscar nomination for playing Louise, but she was first seen as Patrice Kahlman on "A World Apart" and Sara, a murderer on "Search for Tomorrow." Who's she? _____

2. She was nominated for an Oscar for her performance in *An Unmarried Woman*, but she once played Grace Bolton on "Search for Tomorrow." Who's she? _____

3. She left the role of Wendy Wilkins on "Search for Tomorrow" to play the lead in the Broadway production of *Annie*. Who's she? _____

4. He's a major star now, appearing in such movies as *Prelude to a Kiss* and *Glengarry Glen Ross*. His career began on "The Doctors," then he played Joshua Rush on "Knots Landing." Who's he? _____

5. We remember him as Barney Fife, but he was a regular on "Search for Tomorrow" from 1953-55. He played a mute. Who's he? _____

6. She played Jackie Templeton on "General Hospital," but gained greater recognition for her roles in *Indecent Proposal* and *A Few Good Men*. She is _____.

7. She played both Frannie and Sabrina on "As the World Turns,"

but her star is rising from film work in *The Hand That Rocks the Cradle* and *Body of Evidence* (with Madonna).

_____

8. He won an Oscar for *A Fish Called Wanda*, and he was also seen in *The Big Chill*, *Consenting Adults*, and *Silverado*. Once upon a time, though, he was Woody Reed on "Search for Tomorrow."

_____

9. Movie critic Pauline Kael said that he was perhaps the best actor working in America. He costarred in *Driving Miss Daisy* and *Glory*. Perhaps he honed his craft playing Roy Bingham on "Another World." _____

10. He was one of the Mambo Kings, and he also played the rotten-to-the-core husband of Private Benjamin, but on "The Doctors" he was Dr. Mike Powers.

_____

11. He was the sheriff in *Jaws*, Gene Hackman's partner in *The French Connection*, and Bob Fosse in *All That Jazz*. He was also one of several who played Jonas Falk on "Love of Life."

_____

12. Before he became a P.I., he was Jed Andrews on "The Young and the Restless." _____

13. She starred in *Body Heat*, *War of the Roses*, and *Romancing the Stone*. Before that, she was Nola Aldrich on "The Doctors."

_____

14. He's been playing Truman Capote in a one-man show; he won a Tony award for *How to Succeed in Business Without Really Trying*. Before any of that, he was a regular on "The Secret Storm," way back in 1954. _____

15. She went on to a major hit in *When Harry Met Sally*, but she was one of six actresses who have played Betsy on "As the World Turns." Who's she? _____

16. He starred in *Kuffs* and *Heathers;* he was one of Robin Hood's men, and one of the *Young Guns.* He's the kid who reminds everyone of a young Jack Nicholson, and he started out playing D. J. LaSalle on "Ryan's Hope."
Name him. _____

17. This actor (now one of the stars of "Evening Shade") has won acclaim on stage and the big screen, most memorably for his one-man show as Mark Twain. He once played a character named Grayling Dennis on the nearly forgotten soap called "A Brighter Day." Name him. _____

18. He was one of the stars of *Three Men and a Baby*, and he starred in one of TV's most popular sitcoms. In the seventies, however, he played lawyer Tom Conway on "Somerset," a soap of that decade. Name him. _____

19. Another "Somerset" alumnus went on to star in all three of the *Alien* movies. Name her. _____

20. She starred with Mel Gibson in *Forever Young*, but she was once Marty Edison on "Loving." Remember her?

_____

Test Number 1: 99 & 44/100THS% FAMILIAR

1. AMC is **All My Children.**

2. OLTL is **One Life to Live.**

3. GH is **General Hospital.**

4. Y&R is **The Young and the Restless.**

5. AW is **Another World.**

6. ATWT is **As the World Turns.**

7. B&B is **The Bold and the Beautiful.**

8. SB is **Santa Barbara.**

9. FC is **Falcon Crest.**

10. GL is **The Guiding Light.**

Test Number 2: SOAP SATIRE

1. Johnny Carson's version of the soap opera was called **"The Edge of Wetness."**

2. Sally Field and Kevin Kline starred in *Soapdish*.

3. Billy Crystal played a homosexual in **"Soap."**

4. Carol Burnett's version of the soap opera was called **"As the Stomach Turns."**

5. Mary was worried sick about **waxy yellow buildup**.

6. Carol Burnett and Dabney Coleman starred in **"Fresno."**

7. Robert Guillaume played **Benson** in the series of the same name.

8. Named after Mary's cozy small town, this series was called **"Fernwood 2-Night."**

9. David Lynch's creation was called **"Twin Peaks."**

10. The Campbells and the Tates were the two principal families on **"Soap."**

Test Number 3: **SOAP FLAKES**

1. The longest-running soap opera on television is **"The Guiding Light."**

2. **Mary Stuart** played Joanne Gardner Barron Tate Vincente Tourneur on **"Search For Tomorrow."**

3. The cast of **"The Guiding Light"** made *The Cradle Will Fall.*

4. Everybody watched **"General Hospital"** to see the wedding of Luke and Laura.

5. "Like sands through an hour glass, so **are the days of our lives**."

6. **Ivana Trump** played herself on "One Life to Live."

7. The "other woman" in the real-life Trump drama was **Marla Maples**.

8. **"The Donald" (Donald Trump)** himself turned up in a scene with Susan Lucci on "All My Children."

9. **"The Doctors"** was the first daytime soap to win an Emmy.

10. **"Generations"** was the first daytime soap in which one of the major families was black.

11. The "soap within a soap" on "One Life To Live" is **"Fraternity Row."**

12. Dr. Joyce Brothers and Sammy Davis, Jr., both did cameos on **"One Life to Live."**

13. Grant Harrison, Jack Ewing, and Walter Brennan's grandson, Jeff Sonnett were all played by **Dack Rambo**.

14. Brittany Peterson was tried for attempted murder on **"Another World."**

15. **Agnes Nixon** is the veteran soap writer who created "All My Children."

16. **Amnesia** is rare in real life, but quite common among soap opera characters.

17. As of 1993, **Susan Lucci** had still not won an Emmy.

18. **Erica Kane** had the first legal abortion in soap history.

19. **Christina Applegate** first appeared as a babe in her real mother's arms.

20. **David Canary** plays the Chandler twins.

21. **"All My Children"** created these roles for a famous fan, **Carol Burnett**.

22. The granddaughter of Robert Mitchum and the son of John Wayne both appear in **"The Bold and the Beautiful."**

23. It was the theme song from **"The Young and the Restless"** first, but became known as **"Nadia's Theme"** when Nadia Comaneci performed to it during the 1976 Olympics.

24. Steve Ford, son of **Gerald Ford**, played Andy Richards on "The Young and the Restless."

25. "Young Doctor **Malone"** had a twenty-one-year run on radio, and a five-year run on television.

26. Avery Schreiber was once half of the comedy team of **Burns** and Schreiber.

27. Oscar-winning Edna Rae Gilhooley is better known to us as **Ellen Burstyn**.

28. **Kate Jackson** once played Daphne Harridge on "Dark Shadows."

29. **Dame Judith Anderson** played the villainous Minx Lockridge on **"Santa Barbara."**

30. Rodi's Tavern, St. James Church, Giorgio's, the Banner, Wanda's Place, Serenity Springs, and WVLE Radio are **all businesses or places in Llanview, the setting of "One Life to Live."**

31. Happy Homes Bungalows, Cedars Hospital, Spaulding Enterprises, Wheels and Meals, Lewis Oil, and the Regency Hotel are **all places in Springfield, the setting for "Search for Tomorrow."**

32. If you follow the traumas and trials of Lee Ann and Jason, Andrew, Billy, Suede, Luna, Max, Clint, and Sloan, then you're a regular watcher of **"One Life to Live."**

33. If you know all about Clay, Leo, Ava, Christopher, Trisha, Giff, and the McKenzies, then you're hooked on **"Loving."**

34. If Jenna, Alex, Alan-Michael, Harley, Mallet, Blake, and Ross are part of your life, then you've been watching **"The Guiding Light."**

35. Erica, Brian, Dixie, Livia, Lucas, Terence, Taylor, Galen, Carter, and Nurse Marsh are all to be found on **"All My Children."**

36. **(c) Elmer** and **(g) the Marquis de Sade** are not characters on "The Bold and the Beautiful."

37. We all watched and Elizabeth Taylor attended the **"General Hospital"** wedding of **Luke and Laura.**

38. You would have to go to **Pine Valley** to find PVU, the Chateau, the Goal Post, Wildwind, and Cortland Manor.

39. Rory Calhoun starred as Judge Judson Tyler on **"Capitol."**

40. "Ryan's Hope" was **the name of the tavern owned by Johnny Ryan.**

Test Number 4: **SOAP SITES**

1. Henderson: **(e) "Guiding Light"**

2. Springfield: **(q) "Search for Tomorrow"**

3. Pine Valley: **(v) "All My Children"**

4. Genoa City: **(n) "The Young and the Restless"**

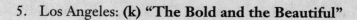

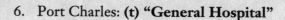
Answers

5. Los Angeles: **(k) "The Bold and the Beautiful"**

6. Port Charles: **(t) "General Hospital"**

7. Chicago: **(s) "Generations"**

8. Barrowsville/Rosehill: **(c) "Love of Life"**

9. Corinth: **(b) "Loving"**

10. Collingsport: **(p) "Dark Shadows"**

11. Salem: **(h) "Days of Our Lives"**

12. Llanview: **(g) "One Life to Live"**

13. Bay City: **(l) "Another World"**

14. Monticello: **(j) "The Edge of Night"**

15. Santa Barbara: **(u) "Santa Barbara"**

16. Oakdale: **(f) "As the World Turns"**

17. Fernwood: **(o) "Mary Hartman, Mary Hartman"**

18. Denver: **(r) "Dynasty"**

19. New Hope: **(a) "Brighter Day"**

20. Woodbridge: **(d) "Secret Storm"**

21. Dunn's River: **(m) "Soap"**

22. San Francisco: **(i) "One Man's Family"**

1. **Susan Sarandon** played Patrice Kahlman and Sara.

2. **Jill Clayburgh** once played Grace Bolton.

3. **Andrea McArdle** left "Search for Tomorrow" to play the lead in *Annie.*

4. **Alec Baldwin** began his career on "The Doctors."

5. We all know **Don Knotts** played Barney Fife.

6. **Demi Moore** was Jackie Templeton.

7. **Julianne Moore** is the rising star from "As the World Turns."

8. Once upon a time, **Kevin Kline** was Woody Reed on "Search for Tomorrow."

9. **Morgan Freeman** was Pauline Kael's choice for the best actor working in America.

10. **Armand Assante** played Dr. Powers.

11. Jonas Falk was played by **Roy Scheider**.

12. **Tom Selleck** was Jed Andrews.

13. **Kathleen Turner** was Nola Aldrich.

14. **Robert Morse** used to be a regular on "The Secret Storm," way back in 1954.

15. **Meg Ryan** was one of the six actresses who have played Betsy.

16. **Christian Slater** started out playing D. J. LaSalle.

17. **Hal Holbrook** was Grayling Dennis on "A Brighter Day."

18. **Ted Danson** once played lawyer Tom Conway on "Somerset."

19. **Sigourney Weaver** is another "Somerset" alumnus.

20. **Isabel Glasser** was once Marty Edison.

There are 102 questions in this section. If you work days and have never become addicted to the soaps, you won't have gotten much of a score on these tests. Soap fans will pity you, and you'll never know what you've been missing—unless you get transferred to the night shift.

Scoring

80–102 Correct: Extremely soapy

40–79 Correct: Light suds

0–39 Correct: No soap

11

Situation Comedies

"We're going to make American families a lot more like the Waltons and a lot less like the Simpsons."

GEORGE BUSH, AUGUST 1992

Nothing is quite as central to the television experience as the sitcom. "Sitcom" does not mean "sitting comatose." It means situation comedy, of course, and television has spawned hundreds of them. No single face says "television" more than the face of Lucille Ball, and her sitcom of the early fifties surely set the tone and much of the style for what was to come. Put identifiable characters in a quirky situation, usually involving a misunderstanding of some kind, and then watch the comedy develop out of the situation. Though Roseanne is surely a grittier version, she's like Lucy in that she faces situations each week, and either finds humor in them or is the butt of humor because of them.

Throughout the history of television, we have taken certain of these characters to our hearts, made them weekly visitors in our homes, were reluctant to let them go even after their series had been canceled. Through syndication and cable, sitcoms that made us laugh as kids are now making our kids laugh.

So, in this chapter, we'll find out how much you know or remember about sitcoms, obscure and familiar, recent and reruns. As a warm-up, we'll start with a little test about "The Beverly Hillbillies." Even if you hated that show, you couldn't avoid seeing it and hearing about it, which means knowing about it. Do you know about it?

Test Number 1: HILLBILLY HEAVEN

You remember the sixties, don't you? Even if you weren't alive then, you've heard about that time ad nauseam—the music, the drugs, the sexual freedom, the Day-Glo colors, the psychedelic clothes. You know, back when the Grateful Dead weren't geriatrics. So, in that time of social and political ferment, of war and rebellion against war, of movements for long-delayed rights, of vast cultural change, what was the most-watched television program? The most-watched television show of the 1960s was (drum roll here) "The Beverly Hillbillies." Does television hold a mirror up to society, or what?

Return with us now to that time of free love, of protest, of a nation losing its innocence; come "listen to my story 'bout a man named Jed, a poor mountaineer barely kept his family fed."

1. Name the place the Beverly Hillbillies moved *away from*.

    _____

2. "The Ballad of Jed Clampett" was a hit record in 1963. It was written and played by _____ and _____ .
    Extra credit if you can name who sang it: _____

3. Cousin Jethro's last name was _____ .

4. Before she was a victim of one of the darker tragedies of the 1960s, she was a regular on "The Beverly Hillbillies" for two years, playing the part of Janet Trego.
   Her name was _____ .

5. This veteran star of his own earlier sitcom was a regular on the show between 1969 and 1971. He played a character named Shifty Shafer. His name was _____ .

6. Mr. Drysdale's assistant was a character named _____ .

7. She was played by _____ .

8. What was Jethro's sister's name? _____ .

9. What did the Clampetts call their swimming pool?
   _____

10. Name Jed's bloodhound. _____

Test Number 2: **CASTING COUCH**

The test that follows is a difficult one. You have to have a long history of watching television to do well at it, but it is meant to be challenging. Can you trace your way through the cast to figure out the sitcom? You'll be lucky, or TV astute, if you get half of these.
Here's the cast. Name the series.

1. *The cast:* Bea Benaderet, Edgar Buchanan, Linda Kaye (Henning), Jeannine Riley, Gunilla Hutton, Meredith MacRae.

   The series? _____

2. *The cast:* Meredith MacRae, Don Grady, William Demarest, Tim Considine, Fred MacMurray, William Frawley.

   The series? _____

3. *The cast:* William Frawley, Desi Arnaz, Lucille Ball, Vivian Vance.

   The series? _____

4. *The cast:* Vivian Vance, Lucille Ball, Jimmy Garrett, Gale Gordon.

   The series? _____

5. *The cast:* Gale Gordon, Eve Arden, Robert Rockwell, Richard Crenna.

   The series? _____

6. *The cast:* Richard Crenna, Kathy Nolan, Michael Winkleman, Walter Brennan.

   The series? _____

7. *The cast:* Walter Brennan, Joyce Menges, Vito Scotti, Susan Neher, Melanie Fullerton, Kay Medford, John Forsythe.

   The series? _____

8. *The cast:* John Forsythe, Noreen Corcoran, Sammee Tong, Bernadette Withers, Jimmy Boyd.

   The series? _____

9. *The cast:* Jimmy Boyd, Kathy Nolan, Joan Staley, Lois Roberts, Edward Andrews, Sheila James, Dick Sargent.

   The series? _____

10. *The cast:* Dick Sargent, Elizabeth Montgomery, Agnes Moorehead.

    The series? _____

11. *The cast:* Cindy Williams, Eddie Mekka, Michael McKean, David L. Lander, Penny Marshall.

    The series? _____

12. *The cast:* Penny Marshall, Jack Klugman, Al Molinaro, Tony Randall.

    The series? _____

13. *The cast:* Tony Randall, Wally Cox, Marion Lorne, Norma Crane, Jack Warden, Ernest Truex.

    The series? _____

14. *The cast:* Ernest Truex, Ann Sothern, Ann Tyrrell, Jack Mullaney, Louis Nye, Ken Berry.

    The series? _____

15. *The cast:* Ken Berry, Vicki Lawrence, Dorothy Lyman, Eric Brown, Rue McClanahan.

    The series? _____

16. *The cast*: Rue McClanahan, Bea Arthur, Betty White, Estelle Getty, Herb Edelman.

    The series? _____

17. *The cast*: Herb Edelman, Rita Moreno, Valerie Curtin, Rachel Dennison, Peter Bonerz.

    The series? _____

18. *The cast:* Peter Bonerz, Suzanne Pleshette, Bill Daily, Bob Newhart.

    The series? _____

19. *The cast:* Bob Newhart, Mary Frann, Tom Poston, Julia Duffy.

    The series? _____

20. *The cast:* Julia Duffy, Annie Potts, Alice Ghostley, Dixie Carter.

    The series? _____

21. *The cast:* Dixie Carter, Gary Coleman, Todd Bridges, Dana Plato, Conrad Bain.

    The series? _____

22. The cast: Conrad Bain, Bill Macy, Adrienne Barbeau, Bea Arthur, Esther Rolle.

    The series? _____

23. The cast: Esther Rolle, Jimmie Walker, Ja'net DuBois, John Amos.

    The series? _____

24. *The cast:* John Amos, Mary Tyler Moore, Ed Asner, Gavin MacLeod, Cloris Leachman, Valerie Harper, Ted Knight.

The series? _____

25. *The cast:* Ted Knight, Nancy Dussault, Deborah Van Valkenburgh, Lydia Cornell, Audrey Meadows.

The series? _____

Test Number 3: NAME, RANK, AND SERIAL NUMBER

No, this test isn't that hard; you don't have to know their serial numbers, but *do you know* the ranks of the following well-known television characters?

1. "Hawkeye" Pierce bore the rank of _____ .

2. Don Rickles played C.P.O. Sharkey.
   That stands for _____ .

3. On "Barney Miller," Wojo held the rank of _____ .

4. On "You'll Never Get Rich," Bilko was, of course, a _____ .

5. Gomer Pyle's long-suffering superior officer was _____ Vince Carter.

6. John MacGillis, played by Gerald McRaney, holds this rank, both at work and at home. _____

7. Barney Fife, of course, held the rank of _____ .

8. "Hot Lips" Houlihan outranked "Hawkeye Pierce."
   She was a _____ .

9. On "McHale's Navy," Tim Conway played Charles Parker, who
      held the rank of

      .

10. "F Troop" featured Wilton Parmenter, a _____ ,
    Morgan O'Rourke, a _____ ,
    and Randolph Agarn, a _____ .

11. Private Benjamin's superior officer was Doreen Lewis. She held
    the rank of _____ .

12. "Police Squad" was headed by Frank Drebin, who held the rank
    of _____ .

Test Number 4: WHERE THE HECK WAS THAT, ANYWAY?

We've traveled far in our video wanderings. Though sedentary, we
began our journeys on Sesame Street, not far from Mr. Rogers'
Neighborhood, just down the block from Captain Kangaroo's place,
across town from Buffalo Bob and his friend Howdy.

As we grew older, we moved and changed friends.

Match the characters with the town or city in which they lived. In
order to increase the difficulty, and to avoid the obvious, I've chosen
secondary characters from the respective situation comedies.

1. Squiggy lived in _____ .   a. Mayberry

2. Lumpy Rutherford lived in _____ . b. Mayfield

3. Jerry Helper lived in _____.   c. Springfield

4. Otis Drexel lived in _____.   d. Brooklyn

5. Bud Anderson lived in _____.   e. New Rochelle

6. Otis Campbell lived in _____.   f. Queens

7. Dennis Mitchell lived in _____.   g. Boulder

8. Nell Harper lived in _____.   h. Milwaukee

9. Principal Skinner lives in _____.   i. Minneapolis

10. Aunt Esther lived in _____.   j. Chicago

11. Mindy McConnell lived in _____.   k. Cincinnati

12. Merle Jeeter lived in _____.   l. Cicely

13. Dr. Joel Fleischman lives in _____.   m. Evening Shade

14. Herman Stiles lives in _____.   n. Indianapolis

15. Trixie Norton lived in _____.   o. St. Louis

16. Julia Sugarbaker lived in _____.   p. Atlanta

17. Ted Baxter lived in _____.   q. Hillsdale

18. Les Nessman lived in _____.   r. Los Angeles

19. Edith Bunker lived in _____.   s. Glen Lawn

20. Dwayne Schneider lived in _____.   t. Fernwood

TV has become increasingly self-referential. Since much of the life we see on TV is meant to reflect the life we lead, TV characters watch TV, too. Not only do TV characters watch TV, but they also sometimes work on TV. The next ten questions all concern shows that had shows built into them. Do you know these shows within shows?

1. On "Home Improvement," comic Tim Allen hosts a fictional show called _____ .

2. On "The Dick Van Dyke Show," Rob, Sally, and Buddy wrote for

    _____ .

3. Bart Simpson's favorite cartoon program is _____ .

4. Murphy Brown is an anchorwoman on a news show called

    _____ .

5. On "WKRP," radio disc jockey Johnny Fever underwent an identity crisis when he moonlighted as host of a TV music show called _____ .

6. Sue Ann Nivens was the host of a show on fictional WJM-TV called _____ .

7. Lucy's husband had his own television show. Lucy was always trying to get on that show.
   What was it? _____

8. The satire of television news on "Saturday Night Live" was called

    _____ .

9. Do-it-yourself book writer and innkeeper Dick Loudon also hosted a local television show called _____ .

10. "The Honeymooners" began as a show within a show, a segment first seen on "Cavalcade of Stars," and then regularly on

_____ .

Test Number 6: STUPID PET TRICKS

If you're really plugged in to your TV, then you not only know the primary and secondary characters on popular and not-so-popular television shows, but you also will know the pets of the primary and secondary characters on those popular and not-so-popular shows. Anyway, let's find out just how much you watched, and how much attention you paid.

Name That Pet!

1. The boys on "My Three Sons" had a dog.
   Name it. _____

2. The Simpsons have a dog.
   Name it. _____

3. The Munsters had a dinosaur.
   Name it. _____

4. The Bundys had a dog.
   Name it. _____

5. The Bradys also had a dog.
   Name it. _____

6. On "The Wonder Years," the Arnolds had a dog.
   Name it. _____

7. On a memorable episode of "WKRP," Herb Tarlek's daughter
   had a pet frog. The frog died.
   Name that frog. _____

8. And the Partridges had a dog.
   Name it. _____

9. In the early days of television, there was a family named Hansen
   on a popular show called "Mama," originally known as "I
   Remember Mama." The Hansens had a dog. Do you remember
   Mama's dog?
   If so, name it. _____

10. Dennis the Menace had a neighbor named Mr. Wilson. Guess
    what? Mr. Wilson had a dog.
    Name it. _____

Test Number 7: **IS IT FOR REAL?**

In the following questions, you will find ten sets of three titles. In each
set, two titles are phonies and one title was actually a network sitcom.
Your job? Pick the one show in each set that was an actual network
show.

1. a. "I'm Shinkwald; He's Lester"

   b. "I'm Rasmussen; He's Arnoldsen"

   c. "I'm Dickens; He's Fenster"

2.   a. "Here's Wacky"

     b. "Here's Boomer"

     c. "Here's Bubba"

3.   a. "Hey Lisa"

     b. "Hey There"

     c. "Hey Jeannie"

4.   a. "Meet Randy"

     b. "Meet Millie"

     c. "Meet the Meathead"

5.   a. "Me and the Chimp"

     b. "Me and the Mongoose"

     c. "Me and the Whale"

6.   a. "Family Madness"

     b. "Family Money"

     c. "Family Matters"

7.   a. "Family Affair"

     b. "Family Values"

     c. "Family Trouble"

8.   a. "Empty Pockets"

     b. "Empty Nest"

     c. "Empty Head"

9. a. "Out of This World"

   b. "Out of Our Heads"

   c. "Out of It"

10. a. "Too Close to Call"

    b. "Too Nice for Words"

    c. "Too Close for Comfort"

Test Number 8: THREE RANDOM QUESTIONS NO TV ADDICT WOULD MISS

1. Maynard Krebs's middle initial? _____

2. Eddie LeBec's occupation? _____

3. Name of the cab company on "Taxi"? _____

You don't often see people working on sitcoms, but when they do, they have bosses, just as in real life. Have you watched enough sitcoms to know who's boss? Try these.

1. Dagwood's boss _____

2. Mary Richards's boss _____

3. Hazel's boss _____

4. Rob Petrie's boss _____

5. Alex Rieger's boss _____

6. Herb Tarlek's boss _____

7. Murphy Brown's boss_____

8. Dobie's boss _____

9. Goober's boss _____

10. George Utley's boss _____

Bonus Test Number 2: MAIDEN NAMES

My daughter, Kelly, gave me this test. I passed it, but just barely. Do you know the married and maiden names of the sitcom characters below? If so, match them up.

Maiden Names	Married Names
1. Rhoda Morgenstern _____	a. Ricardo
2. Sandra Sue Abbott _____	b. Baxter
3. Ann Romano _____	c. Penobscott
4. Shirley Renfro _____	d. Bondurant
5. Lucy MacGillicuddy _____	e. Douglas
6. Margaret Houlihan _____	f. Gerard
7. Carol Kester _____	g. Benson
8. Georgette Franklin _____	h. Partridge
9. Angie Falco _____	i. Bradford
10. Katie Miller _____	j. Cooper

1. Located somewhere in Appalachia, the Beverly Hillbillies moved away from **Bug Tussle**.

2. "The Ballad of Jed Clampett" was written and played by **Lester Flatt and Earl Scruggs** and sung by **Jerry Scoggins**. Flatt and Scruggs appeared on the show from time to time as themselves.

3. Cousin Jethro's last name was **Bodine**. He was played by Max Baer, Jr.

4. Playing a bank secretary, **Sharon Tate** appeared as Janet Trego in the 1963-1964 season.

5. Shifty Shafer was played by **Phil Silvers**, who was the veteran star of "You'll Never Get Rich."

6. Mr. Drysdale's officious assistant was **Jane Hathaway**.

7. She was played by **Nancy Kulp**.

8. Jethro's sister's name was, appropriately enough, **Jethrine**.

9. The Clampetts called their swimming pool **the cement pond.**

10. **Duke** was the name of the family dog.

Test Number 2: **CASTING COUCH**

1. *The cast*: Bea Benaderet, Edgar Buchanan, Linda Kaye (Henning), Jeannine Riley, Gunilla Hutton, Meredith MacRae.

   The series: **"Petticoat Junction"**

Answers

2. *The cast:* Meridith MacRae, Don Grady, William Demarest, Tim Considine, Fred MacMurray, William Frawley.

    The series: **"My Three Sons"**

3. *The cast:* William Frawley, Desi Arnaz, Lucille Ball, Vivian Vance.

    The series: **"I Love Lucy"**

4. *The cast:* Vivian Vance, Lucille Ball, Jimmy Garrett, Gale Gordon.

    The series: **"The Lucy Show"**

5. *The cast:* Gale Gordon, Eve Arden, Robert Rockwell, Richard Crenna.

    The series: **"Our Miss Brooks"**

6. *The cast:* Richard Crenna, Kathy Nolan, Michael Winkelman, Walter Brennan.

    The series: **"The Real McCoys"**

7. *The cast:* Walter Brennan, Joyce Menges, Vito Scotti, Susan Neher, Melanie Fullerton, Kay Medford, John Forsythe.

    The series: **"To Rome With Love"**

8. The cast: John Forsythe, Noreen Corcoran, Sammee Tong, Bernadette Withers, Jimmy Boyd.

    The series: **"Bachelor Father"**

9. *The cast:* Jimmy Boyd, Kathy Nolan, Joan Staley, Lois Roberts, Edward Andrews, Sheila James, Dick Sargent.

   The series: **"Broadside"**

10. *The cast*: Dick Sargent, Elizabeth Montgomery, Agnes Moorehead.

    The series: **"Bewitched"**

11. The cast: Cindy Williams, Eddie Mekka, Michael McKean, David L. Lander, Penny Marshall.

    The series: **"Laverne & Shirley"**

12. *The cast:* Penny Marshall, Jack Klugman, Al Molinaro, Tony Randall.

    The series: **"The Odd Couple"**

13. *The cast*: Tony Randall, Wally Cox, Marion Lorne, Norma Crane, Jack Warden, Ernest Truex.

    The series: **"Mr. Peepers"**

14. *The cast:* Ernest Truex, Ann Sothern, Ann Tyrrell, Jack Mullaney, Louis Nye, Ken Berry.

    The series: **"The Ann Sothern Show"**

15. *The cast:* Ken Berry, Vicki Lawrence, Dorothy Lyman, Eric Brown, Rue McClanahan.

    The series: **"Mama's Family"**

16. *The cast*: Rue McClanahan, Bea Arthur, Betty White, Estelle Getty, Herb Edelman.

    The series: **"The Golden Girls"**

17. *The cast:* Herb Edelman, Rita Moreno, Valerie Curtin, Rachel Dennison, Peter Bonerz.

    The series: **"9 to 5"**

18. *The cast*: Peter Bonerz, Suzanne Pleshette, Bill Daily, Bob Newhart.

    The series: **"The Bob Newhart Show"**

19. The cast: Bob Newhart, Mary Frann, Tom Poston, Julia Duffy.

    The series: **"Newhart"**

20. *The cast*: Julia Duffy, Annie Potts, Alice Ghostley, Dixie Carter.

    The series: **"Designing Women"**

21. *The cast:* Dixie Carter, Gary Coleman, Todd Bridges, Dana Plato, Conrad Bain.

    The series: **"Diff'rent Strokes"**

22. *The cast*: Conrad Bain, Bill Macy, Adrienne Barbeau, Bea Arthur, Esther Rolle.

    The series: **"Maude"**

23. *The cast:* Esther Rolle, Jimmie Walker, Ja'net DuBois, John Amos.

    The series: **"Good Times"**

24. *The cast:* John Amos, Mary Tyler Moore, Ed Asner, Gavin MacLeod, Cloris Leachman, Valerie Harper, and Ted Knight.

   The series: **"The Mary Tyler Moore Show"**

25. *The cast:* Ted Knight, Nancy Dussault, Deborah Van Valkenburgh, Lydia Cornell, Audrey Meadows.

   The series: **"Too Close for Comfort"**

Test Number 3: NAME, RANK, AND SERIAL NUMBER

1. Alan Alda played **Captain** Benjamin Franklin "Hawkeye" Pierce.

2. Don Rickles was C.P.O. Otto Sharkey, a naval **Chief Petty Officer**.

3. Wojo was a **sergeant**.

4. Bilko was a **sergeant**.

5. Gomer's platoon leader was **Sergeant** Carter.

6. Gerald McRaney plays Marine **Major** "Mac" MacGillis in "Major Dad."

7. Sheriff Taylor's cousin Barney was Mayberry's **deputy sheriff**.

8. Loretta Swit played **Major** Margaret Houlihan.

9. Tim Conway was the bungling **Ensign** Parker.

10. Ken Berry played **Captain** Parmenter, Forrest Tucker was **Sergeant** O'Rourke, and Larry Storch was **Corporal** Agarn.

11. Eileen Brennan played the frustrated **Captain** Lewis.

12. Leslie Nielsen played Frank Drebin, whose rank varied from **sergeant** to **lieutenant**, depending on how his luck was holding out.

Answers

Test Number 4: **WHERE THE HECK WAS THAT, ANYWAY?**

1. Squiggy lived in **(h) Milwaukee.**

2. Lumpy Rutherford lived in **(b) Mayfield.**

3. Jerry Helper lived in **(e) New Rochelle.**

4. Otis Drexel lived in **(o) St. Louis.**

5. Bud Anderson lived in **(c) Springfield.**

6. Otis Campbell lived in **(a) Mayberry.**

7. Dennis Mitchell lived in **(q) Hillsdale.**

8. Nell Harper lived in **(s) Glen Lawn.**

9. Principal Skinner lives in **(c) Springfield.**

10. Aunt Esther lived in **(r) Los Angeles.**

11. Mindy McConnell lived in **(g) Boulder.**

12. Merle Jeeter lived in **(t) Fernwood.**

13. Dr. Joel Fleischman lives in **(l) Cicely.**

14. Herman Stiles lives in **(m) Evening Shade.**

15. Trixie Norton lived in **(d) Brooklyn.**

16. Julia Sugarbaker lived in **(p) Atlanta**.

17. Ted Baxter lived in **(i) Minneapolis**.

18. Les Nessman lived in **(k) Cincinnati**.

19. Edith Bunker lived in **(f) Queens**.

20. Dwayne Schneider lived in **(n) Indianapolis**.

Test Number 5: SHOWS WITHIN SHOWS

1. Tim Allen hosts **"Tool Time."**

2. Rob, Sally, and Buddy wrote for **"The Alan Brady Show."**

3. Bart's favorite cartoon program is **"The Itchy and Scratchy Show."**

4. Murphy anchors **"F.Y.I."**

5. Dr. Johnny moonlighted as host of **"Dance Fever."**

6. Sue Ann's show was called **"The Happy Homemaker."**

7. Ricky's television show was **"The Ricky Ricardo Show."**

8. The satire of TV news on "Saturday Night Live" was called **"Weekend Update."**

9. Dick Loudon hosted **"Vermont Today."**

10. "The Honeymooners" was regularly seen on **"The Jackie Gleason Show."**

1. Mike, Robbie, and Chip had a dog named **Tramp**.

2. Bart's best friend is **Santa's Little Helper**.

3. **Spot** was the Munster family's pet dinosaur.

4. **Buck** was the Bundys' dog.

5. The six Brady children had a dog named **Tiger**.

6. **Buster** was the Arnold family's pet pooch.

7. **Green Peace** was the name of the Tarleks' ill-fated frog.

8. The Partridge family pet was **Simone**.

9. The Hansens' dog was named **Willie**.

10. Mr. Wilson's furry friend was named **Fremont**.

Test Number 7: IS IT FOR REAL?

1. **(c) "I'm Dickens; He's Fenster"** is the real show.

2. **(b) "Here's Boomer"** is the real show.

3. **(c) "Hey Jeannie"** is the real show.

4. **(b) "Meet Millie"** is the real show.

5. **(a) "Me and the Chimp"** is the real show.

6. **(c) "Family Matters"** is the real show.

7. **(a) "Family Affair"** is the real show.

8. **(b) "Empty Nest"** is the real show.

9. **(a) "Out of This World"** is the real show.

10. **(c) "Too Close for Comfort"** is the real show.

Answers

Test Number 8: THREE RANDOM QUESTIONS NO TV ADDICT WOULD MISS

1. Maynard Krebs's middle initial was **G.**

2. Eddie LeBec was **a professional hockey player, and then he was in an ice show.**

3. The cabbies on "Taxi" worked for **The Sunshine Cab Company.**

Bonus Test: WHO'S THE BOSS?

1. Dagwood's boss was **Mr. Dithers**.

2. Mary's boss was, of course, **Lou Grant**.

3. Hazel's boss was **Mr. B. (for Baxter).**

4. Rob Petrie's boss was **Alan Brady**.

5. Alex Rieger worked for **Louie DePalma**.

6. Herb Tarlek worked for **"The Big Guy," Mr. Carlson**.

7. Murphy Brown is supervised, sort of, by **Miles Silverberg**.

8. Dobie worked for his father, **Herbert T. Gillis**, at the store.

9. Goober worked for **Wally** down at the filling station.

10. George Utley worked for **Dick Loudon** at the Stratford Inn.

Bonus Test Number 2: **MAIDEN NAMES**

1. Rhoda Morgenstern: **(f) Gerard**

2. Sandra Sue Abbott: **(i) Bradford**

3. Ann Romano: **(j) Cooper**

4. Shirley Renfro: **(h) Partridge**

5. Lucy MacGillicuddy:**(a) Ricardo**

6. Margaret Houlihan: **(c) Penobscott**

7. Carol Kester: **(d) Bondurant**

8. Georgette Franklin: **(b) Baxter**

9. Angie Falco: **(g) Benson**

10. Katie Miller: **(e) Douglas**

So what's the situation with your performance on this test? Is it a comedy? Or is it a triumph? There were 120 questions. Even a casual viewer would have gotten more than half of them.

Anyway, check your S.C.A.T. (Situation Comedy Aptitude Test) scores.

Scoring

80–120 Correct: "Hi, honey, I'm home free."

40–79 Correct: Moderate viewer.

0–39 Correct: You never liked sitcoms, and you probably never will. Either that, or you don't own a TV.

12

What a Character!

"My character is not a strong, integral part of the story. In fact, I'm kind of surprised that the lack of information that's been written about Kramer has somehow created a mystique for the character. I mean, they've never even shown the inside of my apartment. Then again, you never really saw Norton's apartment in 'The Honeymooners.'"

MICHAEL RICHARDS, KRAMER ON "SEINFELD"

One fundamental pleasure of stories is to be found in the characters we encounter in them. Television has given us countless stories populated by even more characters. Some of those characters have been tissue-thin, one-dimensional, and not much worth our attention. But many of them have been quite memorable, even those characterized only by a few idiosyncrasies.

Which of these characters do *you* remember? If you do remember them, surely you can provide the name of the show in which you made their acquaintance.

1. A photographer with the nickname Animal
    _____

2. A prankster bar owner named Gary _____

3. Aunt Esther _____

4. A tipsy doorman named Carlton _____

5. Officer Swanhouser (Swanny) and Officer Smith (Smitty)
    _____

6. A hired hand named Pepino _____

7. A musical family named Darling _____

8. A gravelly-voiced court officer named Hacker _____

9. Colonel Klink, Commandant _____

10. A Latino gardener named Fronk _____

11. Crazy Guggenheim _____

12. Willie Lump Lump _____

13. Edith Ann _____

14. Two Wild and Crazy Guys _____

15. The Pigeon Sisters _____

16. Maurice, a warlock father _____

17. Howard, nutty-neighbor navigator _____

18. Maynard G. Krebs, kook _____

19. Dapper Gordon Hathaway, who said, "Hi-ho, Steverino"
    _____

20. Leigh French, who invited us to "Take a little tea with Goldie"
    _____

21. Mr. Tudball and Mrs. Wiggins _____

22. Engineer Charlie Pratt, played by Smiley Burnette _____

23. Reuben Kincaid, manager _____

24. Charlie Halper, owner of the Copa _____

25. Major Charles Emerson Winchester, played by David Ogden
    Stiers _____

26. A photographer's assistant nicknamed "Schultzy" _____

27. Aunt Blabby _____

28. Kramer, oddball neighbor _____

29. A gay boss named Leon _____

30. Principal Grace _____

31. "The Happy Homemaker" _____

32. Wanna-be country singer Loretta Haggers _____

33. A crude shoe salesman named Al _____

34. Man-hungry Blanche Devereaux _____

35. Always agitated Sergeant Vince Carter _____

36. Two southern interior decorators named Dixie and Allison

    _____

37. Long-suffering next-door neighbor, George Wilson _____

38. Wrangler Jane, mad for the captain _____

39. Tootie, with the braces _____

40. Nerdy Arvid Engen _____

41. "Dy-no-mite" was the phrase, J.J. was the character. Now what was the series? _____

42. Thurston Howell III _____

43. Frank Parrish, who inherited Chez Louisiane _____

44. Reverend LeRoy _____

45. Krusty the Clown _____

46. His nickname is Wiz; he has a bladder problem on _____

47. Paul Pfeiffer, Kevin's nerdy friend _____

48. Jane Hathaway, Mr. Drysdale's secretary _____

49. Would-be swinger, Ralph Furley _____

50. He's John, he's overbearing, and he owns Melville's. _____

51. Art Fern, sleazy late-night pitch man _____

52. Jennifer, a not-dumb blond receptionist _____

53. An aging Alaska bar owner with a young wife _____

54. Larry "Bud" Melman _____

55. Blaine Edwards and Antoine Mayweather, film critics _____

56. Newspaper columnist in love _____

57. White DJ, black radio station _____

58. Wanna-be country singer working as waitress _____

59. He said "Shazam" all the time. _____

60. Anchorwoman who loves the Motown sound _____

61. Bandleader's wife who wants in the act _____

62. Levitt, too short to be a detective _____

63. The Church Lady _____

64. Uncle Tonoose _____

65. Rochester, the valet _____

66. An idiot detective named Drebin _____

67. Dweeby Ensign Parker _____

68. Cockroach, Theo's friend _____

69. The Nairobi Trio _____

70. Uncle Bub, and then Uncle Charley, lovable curmudgeons
_____

71. A faithful Indian companion _____

72. Compulsive liar Tommy Flanagan _____

73. Yemana, world's worst coffee maker _____

74. Al, Tim's surly helper _____

75. The Hickenloopers, battling spouses _____

76. Pat Paulsen, perennial presidential candidate _____

77. Jessica Fletcher, amateur sleuth _____

78. Dr. Tooth & the Electric Mayhem _____

79. Arnold Horshack, nerd _____

80. John Beresford Tipton, eccentric rich guy _____

81. A deputy with a limp and a drawl _____

82. The Poor Soul _____

83. Detective George Francisco, Tenctonian birth-giver _____

84. Lieutenant Commander Data, would-be human _____

85. Gracie, ditzy wife _____

86. George Utley, not-too-bright handyman _____

87. The Log Lady _____

88. Mike Nelson, underwater hero _____

89. Dr. Mark Craig, ego-driven surgeon _____

90. Private Duane Doberman, ill-kempt, overweight GI
    _____

91. Walter Denton, not-bright student whose voice was changing
    _____

92. Ed Norton, double-jointed sewer worker _____

93. "Boss" Hogg, corrupt sheriff _____

94. Herb Philbrick, commie hunter _____

95. Forrest Bedford, Bryland's prosecutor _____

96. Bill Bittinger, rotten TV talk show host _____

97. Boris Badenov, cartoon villain _____

98. Robert McCall, one-man security force _____

99. The Bradley clan, of Hooterville _____

100. Lucas McCain, frontier single parent _____

Match the doctor to the show.

1. Dr. Alex Stone _____   a. "Quantum Leap"

2. Dr. Steven Kiley _____   b. "Medical Center"

3. Dr. David Zorba _____   c. "The Love Boat"

4. Dr. John McIntyre _____   d. "Cheers"

5. Dr. Konrad Styner _____   e. "The Cosby Show"

6. Dr. Joe Gannon _____   f. "Doc"

7. Dr. Joe Bogert _____   g. "Evening Shade"

8. Dr. Adam Bricker _____   h. "Growing Pains"

9. Dr. Joel Fleischman _____   i. "Trapper John"

10. Dr. Sam Beckett _____   j. "Marcus Welby, M.D."

11. Dr. Cliff Huxtable _____   k. "Gunsmoke"

12. Dr. Galen Adams _____   l. "Medic"

13. Dr. Jason Seaver _____   m. "Northern Exposure"

14. Dr. Harlan Elldridge _____   n. "Ben Casey"

15. Dr. Lilith Sternin _____   o. "The Donna Reed Show"

16. Dr. Richard Kimble _____   p. "The Fugitive"

17. Dr. Donald Westphall _____   q. "China Beach"

18. Dr. Joe Martin _____   r. "Dr. Kildare"

19. Dr. Leonard Gillespie _____ s. "All My Children"

20. Dr. Dick Richard _____   t. "St. Elsewhere"

Test Number 3: **MAKE TIME FOR SERGEANTS**

Match the sergeant to the series.

1. Sgt. "Pepper" Anderson _____   a. "F Troop"

2. Sgt. Ernie Bilko _____   b. "Felony Squad"

3. Sgt. Chip Saunders _____   c. "Dragnet"

4. Sgt. Hans Schultz _____   d. "Police Woman"

5. Sgt. Vince Carter _____   e. "You'll Never Get Rich"

6. Det. Sgt. Sam Stone _____   f. "Combat"

7. Sgt. Morgan O'Rourke _____   g. "Hogan's Heroes"

8. Sgt. Phil Esterhaus _____   h. "CHiPs"

9. Sgt. Joe Friday _____   i. "Hill Street Blues"

10. Sgt. Joe Getraer _____   j. "Gomer Pyle, U.S.M.C."

Match the legal eagle to the series.

1. Lawrence and Ken Preston, father and son _____

2. Assistant DA Dan Fielding _____

3. Joyce Davenport, public defender _____

4. Judge Joseph Wapner _____

5. District Attorney Hamilton Burger _____

6. Law firm of McKenzie, Brackman, Chaney, and Kuzak. _____

7. Assistant DA Julie March _____

8. Algonquin J. Calhoun _____

9. Assistant DA Ben Stone _____

10. Clair Huxtable _____

a. "Hill Street Blues"

b. "L.A. Law"

c. "The Cosby Show"

d. "Night Court"

e. "Law and Order"

f. "People's Court"

g. "Matlock"

h. "The Defenders"

i. "Perry Mason"

j. "Amos and Andy"

Test Number 5: "SATURDAY NIGHT LIVE"

"Saturday Night Live" has given us many memorable characters and left an indelible stamp on American popular culture. Even if you don't watch the show, you probably know of some of these characters. Match the "Saturday Night Live" character to the cast member who made that character memorable.

1. Baba Wawa _____

2. Father Guido Sarducci _____

3. Buckwheat _____

4. Roseanne Roseannadanna _____

5. The Church Lady _____

6. Fernando _____

7. Deiter on "Sprockets" _____

8. The Samurai Tailor _____

9. The Master Thespian _____

10. Ed Grimley _____

11. Gumby _____

12. The Land Shark _____

13. Mr. Robinson _____

14. Emily Litella _____

a. John Belushi

b. Dana Carvey

c. Jon Lovitz

d. Billy Crystal

e. Martin Short

f. Steve Martin

g. Dan Aykroyd

h. Lorraine Newman

i. Eddie Murphy

j. Don Novello

k. Mike Myers

l. Jane Curtin

m. Bill Murray

n. Kevin Nealon

15. Lisa Lubner _____   o. Nora Dunn

16. Mrs. Lubner _____   p. Chevy Chase

17. Tod, Lisa's boyfriend _____   q. Gilda Radner

18. King Tut _____

19. Bass-O-Matic salesman _____

20. Pat Stevens _____

Test Number 6: PARENTS AND THEIR OFFSPRING

In the test that follows, match the moms and dads with their fictional children.

1. Al and Peg Bundy _____   a. Maggie

2. Danny Williams _____   b. Lamont

3. Archie and Edith Bunker _____   c. Jackie

4. Samantha and Darrin
   Stephens _____   d. Julie

5. Ann Romano _____   e. Rusty

6. Alice Hyatt _____   f. Rudy

7. Fred and Lily Munster _____   g. Richie

8. Howard and Marion
   Cunningham _____   h. Mearth

9. Steve and Elyse Keaton _____   i. Becky

10. Fred Sanford _____   j. Corky

11. Henry and Muriel Rush _____   k. Malory

12. Homer and Marge Simpson _____   l. Casey

13. Drew and Libby Thatcher _____   m. Bess

14. Jack and Norma Arnold _____   n. Tommy

15. Cliff and Clair Huxtable _____   o. Tabitha

16. Dan and Roseanne Conner _____   p. Eddie

17. Andy Taylor _____   q. Kevin

18. Mac and Polly MacGillis _____   r. Gloria

19. Phyllis Lindstrom _____   s. Kelly

20. Mork and Mindy _____   t. Opie

Test Number 7: FUN COUPLES

Lovers, buddies, husbands and wives. Television has given us couples
who are forever linked in our memories. Or at least some of them are.
Can you make the linkages? In the test below, match the couples.

1. Ralph Kramden _____   a. Samantha

2. Dobie Gillis _____   b. Roseanne

3. Cliff Huxtable _____   c. Ann Marie

4. Dan Conner _____   d. Laura

5. Sam Malone _____   e. Lou Ann Povey

6. Ward Cleaver _____   f. Maddie Hayes

7. Barney Fife _____   g. Lily

8. Gomer Pyle _____   h. Sue Ellen

9. David Addison _____   i. Diane Chambers

10. Gomez Addams _____   j. Vera

11. Fred Munster _____   k. Thalia Menninger

12. Norm Peterson _____   l. Clair

13. Don Hollinger _____   m. June

14. Darrin Stephens _____   n. Thelma Lou

15. J. R. Ewing _____   o. Morticia

16. Rob Petrie _____   p. Alice

17. Dick Loudon _____   q. Kitty

18. Bob Hartley _____   r. Mary

19. Matt Dillon __   s. Joanna

20. Tom Hartman __   t. Emily

What a Character! 235

1. A photographer with the nickname "Animal": **"Lou Grant"**

2. A prankster bar owner named Gary: **"Cheers"**

3. Aunt Esther: **"Sanford and Son"**

4. A tipsy doorman named Carlton: **"Rhoda"**

5. Officer Swanhouser (Swanny) and Officer Smith (Smitty): **"Sanford and Son"**

6. A hired hand named Pepino: **"The Real McCoys"**

7. A musical family named Darling: **"The Andy Griffith Show"**

8. A gravelly-voiced court officer named Hacker: **"Night Court"**

9. Colonel Klink, Commandant: **"Hogan's Heroes"**

10. A Latino gardener named Fronk: **"Father Knows Best"**

11. Crazy Guggenheim: **"The Jackie Gleason Show"**

12. Willie Lump Lump: **"The Red Skelton Show"**

13. Edith Ann: **"Rowan and Martin's Laugh-In"**

14. Two Wild and Crazy Guys: **"Saturday Night Live"**

15. The Pigeon Sisters: **"The Odd Couple"**

16. Maurice, a warlock father: **"Bewitched"**

17. Howard, nutty-neighbor navigator: **"The Bob Newhart Show"**

18. Maynard G. Krebs, kook: **"The Many Loves of Dobie Gillis"**

19. Dapper Gordon Hathaway, who said, "Hi-ho, Steverino": **"The Steve Allen Comedy Hour"**

20. Leigh French, who invited us to "Take a little tea with Goldie": **"The Smothers Brothers Comedy Hour"**

21. Mr. Tudball and Mrs. Wiggins: **"The Carol Burnett Show"**

22. Engineer Charlie Pratt, played by Smiley Burnette: **"Petticoat Junction"**

23. Reuben Kincaid, manager: **"The Partridge Family"**

24. Charlie Halper, owner of the Copa: **"The Danny Thomas Show"**

25. Major Charles Emerson Winchester, played by David Ogden Stiers: **"M*A*S*H"**

26. A photographer's assistant nicknamed "Schultzy": **"The Bob Cummings Show"**

27. Aunt Blabby: **"The Tonight Show"**

28. Kramer, oddball neighbor: **"Seinfeld"**

29. A gay boss named Leon: **"Roseanne"**

30. Principal Grace: **"Parker Lewis Can't Lose"**

31. "The Happy Homemaker": **"The Mary Tyler Moore Show"**

32. Wanna-be country singer Loretta Haggers: **"Mary Hartman, Mary Hartman"**

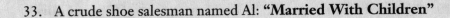

33. A crude shoe salesman named Al: **"Married With Children"**

34. Man-hungry Blanche Devereaux: **"Golden Girls"**

35. Always agitated Sergeant Vince Carter: **"Gomer Pyle, U.S.M.C."**

36. Two southern interior decorators named Dixie and Allison: **"Designing Women"**

37. Long-suffering next-door neighbor, George Wilson: **"Dennis the Menace"**

38. Wrangler Jane, mad for the captain: **"F Troop"**

39. Tootie, with the braces: **"Facts of Life"**

40. Nerdy Arvid Engen: **"Head of the Class"**

41. "Dy-no-mite" was the phrase, J.J. was the character: **"Good Times"** was the series.

42. Thurston Howell III: **"Gilligan's Island"**

43. Frank Parrish, who inherited Chez Louisiane: **"Frank's Place"**

44. Reverend LeRoy: **"The Flip Wilson Show"**

45. Krusty the Clown: **"The Simpsons"**

46. His nickname is Wiz; he has a bladder problem on: **"Roc"**

47. Paul Pfeiffer, Kevin's nerdy friend: **"The Wonder Years"**

48. Jane Hathaway, Mr. Drysdale's secretary: **"The Beverly Hillbillies"**

49. Would-be swinger Ralph Furley: **"Three's Company"**

50. He's John, he's overbearing, and he owns Melville's: **"Cheers"**

51. Art Fern, sleazy late-night pitch man: **"The Tonight Show"**

52. Jennifer, a not-dumb blond receptionist: **"WKRP"**

53. An aging Alaska bar owner with a young wife: **"Northern Exposure"**

54. Larry "Bud" Melman: **"Late Night With David Letterman"**

55. Blaine Edwards and Antoine Mayweather, film critics: **"In Living Color"**

56. Newspaper columnist in love: **"Love and War"**

57. White DJ, black radio station: **"Rhythm & Blues"**

58. Wanna-be country singer working as waitress: **"Delta"**

59. He said "Shazam" all the time: **"The Andy Griffith Show"**

60. Anchorwoman who loves the Motown sound: **"Murphy Brown"**

61. Bandleader's wife who wants in the act: **"I Love Lucy"**

62. Levitt, too short to be a detective: **"Barney Miller"**

63. The Church Lady: **"Saturday Night Live"**

64. Uncle Tonoose: **"The Danny Thomas Show"**

65. Rochester, the valet: **"The Jack Benny Show"**

66. An idiot detective named Drebin: **"Police Squad"**

67. Dweeby Ensign Parker: **"McHale's Navy"**

68. Cockroach, Theo's friend: **"The Bill Cosby Show"**

69. The Nairobi Trio: **"The Ernie Kovacs Show"**

70. Uncle Bub, and then Uncle Charley, lovable curmudgeons: **"My Three Sons"**

71. A faithful Indian companion: **"The Lone Ranger"**

72. Compulsive liar Tommy Flanagan: **"Saturday Night Live"**

73. Yemana, world's worst coffee maker: **"Barney Miller"**

74. Al, Tim's surly helper: **"Home Improvement"**

75. The Hickenloopers, battling spouses: **"Your Show of Shows"**

76. Pat Paulsen, perennial presidential candidate: **"The Smothers Brothers Comedy Hour"**

77. Jessica Fletcher, amateur sleuth: **"Murder, She Wrote"**

78. Dr. Tooth & the Electric Mayhem: **"The Muppet Show"**

79. Arnold Horshack, nerd: **"Welcome Back, Kotter"**

80. John Beresford Tipton, eccentric rich guy: **"The Millionaire"**

81. A deputy with a limp and a drawl: **"Gunsmoke"**

82. The Poor Soul: **"The Jackie Gleason Show"**

83. Detective George Francisco, Tenctonian birth-giver: **"Alien Nation"**

84. Lieutenant Commander Data, would-be human: **"Star Trek, the Next Generation"**

85. Gracie, ditzy wife: **"The George Burns and Gracie Allen Show"**

86. George Utley, not-too-bright handyman: **"Newhart"**

87. The Log Lady: **"Twin Peaks"**

88. Mike Nelson, underwater hero: **"Sea Hunt"**

89. Dr. Mark Craig, ego-driven surgeon: **"St. Elsewhere"**

90. Private Duane Doberman, ill-kempt, overweight GI: **"You'll Never Get Rich"**

91. Walter Denton, not-bright student whose voice was changing: **"Our Miss Brooks"**

92. Ed Norton, double-jointed sewer worker: **"The Honeymooners"**

93. "Boss" Hogg, corrupt sheriff: **"The Dukes of Hazzard"**

94. Herb Philbrick, commie hunter: **"I Led Three Lives"**

95. Forrest Bedford, Bryland's prosecutor: **"I'll Fly Away"**

96. Bill Bittinger, rotten TV talk show host: **"Buffalo Bill"**

97. Boris Badenov, cartoon villain: **"The Bullwinkle Show"**

98. Robert McCall, one-man security force: **"The Equalizer"**

99. The Bradley clan, of Hooterville: **"Petticoat Junction"**

100. Lucas McCain, frontier single parent: **"The Rifleman"**

Test Number 2: **IS THERE A DOCTOR IN THE HOUSE?**

1. Dr. Alex Stone: **(o) "The Donna Reed Show"**

2. Dr. Steven Kiley: **(j) "Marcus Welby, M.D."**

3. Dr. David Zorba: **(n) "Ben Casey"**

4. Dr. John McIntyre: **(i) "Trapper John"**

5. Dr. Konrad Styner: **(l) "Medic"**

6. Dr. Joe Gannon: **(b) "Medical Center""**

7. Dr. Joe Bogert: **(f) "Doc"**

8. Dr. Adam Bricker: **(c) "The Love Boat"**

9. Dr. Joel Fleischman: **(m) "Northern Exposure"**

10. Dr. Sam Beckett: **(a) "Quantum Leap"**

11. Dr. Cliff Huxtable: **(e) "The Cosby Show"**

12. Dr. Galen Adams: **(k) "Gunsmoke"**

13. Dr. Jason Seaver: **(h) "Growing Pains"**

14. Dr. Harlan Elldridge: **(g) "Evening Shade"**

15. Dr. Lilith Sternin: **(d) "Cheers"**

16. Dr. Richard Kimble: **(p) "The Fugitive"**

17. Dr. Donald Westphall: **(t) "St. Elsewhere"**

18. Dr. Joe Martin: **(s) "All My Children"**

19. Dr. Leonard Gillespie: **(r) "Dr. Kildare"**

20. Dr. Dick Richard: **(q) "China Beach"**

Answers

Test Number 3: **MAKE TIME FOR SERGEANTS**

1. Sgt. "Pepper" Anderson: **(d) "Police Woman"**

2. Sgt. Ernie Bilko: **(e) "You'll Never Get Rich"**

3. Sgt. Chip Saunders: **(f) "Combat"**

4. Sgt. Hans Schultz: **(g) "Hogan's Heroes"**

5. Sgt. Vince Carter: **(j) "Gomer Pyle, U.S.M.C."**

6. Det. Sgt. Sam Stone: **(b) "Felony Squad"**

7. Sgt. Morgan O'Rourke: **(f) "Combat"**

8. Sgt. Phil Esterhaus: **(i) "Hill Street Blues"**

9. Sgt. Joe Friday: **(c) "Dragnet"**

10. Sgt. Joe Getraer: **(h) "CHiPS"**

Answers

1   Lawrence and Ken Preston, father and son: **(h) "The Defenders"**

2. Assistant DA Dan Fielding: **(d) "Night Court"**

3. Joyce Davenport, public defender: **(a) "Hill Street Blues"**

4. Judge Joseph Wapner: **(f) "People's Court"**

5. District Attorney Hamilton Burger: **(i) "Perry Mason"**

6. Law firm of McKenzie, Brackman, Chaney, and Kuzak: **(b) "L.A. Law"**

7. Assistant DA Julie March: **(g) "Matlock"**

8. Algonquin J. Calhoun: **(j) "Amos and Andy"**

9. Assistant DA Ben Stone: **(e) "Law and Order"**

10. Clair Huxtable: **(c) "The Cosby Show"**

Test Number 5: "SATURDAY NIGHT LIVE"

1. Baba Wawa: **(q) Gilda Radner**

2. Father Guido Sarducci: **(j) Don Novello**

3. Buckwheat: **(i) Eddie Murphy**

4. Roseanne Roseannadanna: **(q) Gilda Radner**

5. The Church Lady: **(b) Dana Carvey**

6. Fernando: **(d) Billy Crystal**

7. Deiter on "Sprockets": **(k) Mike Meyrs**

8. The Samurai Tailor: **(a) John Belushi**

9. The Master Thespian: **(c) Jon Lovitz**

10. Ed Grimley: **(e) Martin Short**

11. Gumby: **(i) Eddie Murphy**

12. The Land Shark: **(p) Chevy Chase**

13. Mr. Robinson: **(i) Eddie Murphy**

14. Emily Litella: **(q) Gilda Radner**

15. Lisa Lubner: **(q) Gilda Radner**

16. Mrs. Lubner: **(l) Jane Curtin**

17. Tod, Lisa's boyfriend: **(m) Bill Murray**

18. King Tut: **(f) Steve Martin**

19. Bass-O-Matic salesman: **(g) Dan Aykroyd**

20. Pat Stevens: **(o) Nora Dunn**

Answers

1.   Al and Peg Bundy: **(s) Kelly**

2.   Danny Williams: **(e) Rusty**

3.   Archie and Edith Bunker: **(r) Gloria**

4.   Samantha and Darrin Stephens: **(o) Tabitha**

5.   Ann Romano: **(d) Julie**

6.   Alice Hyatt: **(n) Tommy**

7.   Fred and Lily Munster: **(p) Eddie**

8.   Howard and Marion Cunningham: **(g) Richie**

9.   Steve and Elyse Keaton: **(k) Malory**

10.   Fred Sanford: **(b) Lamont**

11.   Henry and Muriel Rush: **(c) Jackie**

12.   Homer and Marge Simpson: **(a) Maggie**

13.   Drew and Libby Thatcher: **(j) Corky**

14.   Jack and Norma Arnold: **(q) Kevin**

15.   Cliff and Clair Huxtable: **(f) Rudy**

16.   Dan and Roseanne Conner: **(i) Becky**

17.   Andy Taylor: **(t) Opie**

18. Mac and Polly MacGillis: **(l) Casey**

19. Phyllis Lindstrom: **(m) Bess**

20. Mork and Mindy: **(h) Mearth**

Test Number 7: FUN COUPLES

1. Ralph Kramden: **(p) Alice**

2. Dobie Gillis: **(k) Thalia Menninger**

3. Cliff Huxtable: **(l) Clair**

4. Dan Conner: **(b) Roseanne**

5. Sam Malone: **(i) Diane Chambers**

6. Ward Cleaver: **(m) June**

7. Barney Fife: **(n) Thelma Lou**

8. Gomer Pyle: **(e) Lou Ann Povey**

9. David Addison: **(f) Maddie Hayes**

10. Gomez Addams: **(o) Morticia**

11. Fred Munster: **(g) Lily**

12. Norm Peterson: **(j) Vera**

13. Don Hollinger: **(c) Ann Marie**

14. Darrin Stephens: **(a) Samantha**

15. J. R. Ewing: **(h) Sue Ellen**

16. Rob Petrie: **(d) Laura**

17. Dick Loudon: **(s) Joanna**

18. Bob Hartley: **(t) Emily**

19. Matt Dillon: **(q) Kitty**

20. Tom Hartman: **(r) Mary**

If there were memorable TV characters I haven't included in this test, then I apologize for that. I'd be curious to know who you remember that I've forgotten. It's a bit like school, where we sometimes learned fascinating things that were not covered at exam time.

Did you have an eye for characters—and a retentive memory?

There are two hundred questions in this set of tests. Any regular TV viewer would have gotten at least half of them. Fewer than that, and you're spending too much time away from your television set. Either that, or you have a severe memory deficiency.

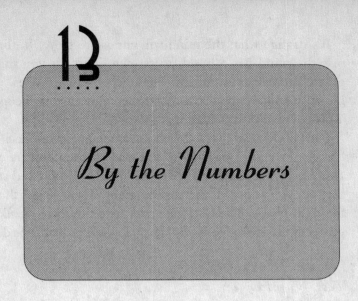

13

By the Numbers

I don't want to discourage anyone, but the test that follows is a difficult one, and you might want to have a pocket calculator at hand when you take it. The answer to each question is expressed in the form of a number, and your task here is to make the numbers add up. Some of those numbers are big ones. If you're the sort of person who likes a challenge, then this test is for you. If you're the sort of person who likes math puzzles, then you, too, should like this test.

So, how's your memory for numbers? Do you remember the combination to your high school locker? Do you remember the phone number of that special someone from several years ago even though the name just slips your mind? Can you rattle off your driver's license number when you cash a check, or do you have to look each time?

It's strange what the mind will choose to store. In the realm of memory, the mind has a mind of its own. Though you might forget some pretty important numbers (birthdays, anniversaries, your credit card limit), it's likely that you remember quite a few inconsequential ones. This is a test of that memory.

Each of the tests that follow features ten questions. Each answer is a number. At the end of each set of ten, add up the numbers contained in your answers. If your number matches the number announced at the beginning of that set, you've got all the answers right, if you've got the right answers in the right places. The tests get easier (and the totals smaller) as the chapter proceeds, so don't give up. By the end, you'll probably be doing a bit better.

Test Number 1:

Fill in the correct answers below and your total will be 40,657.

1. The "M*A*S*H" unit was number _____.

2. The prefix used for nearly all
   fictional phone numbers on television is _____.

3. Joe Friday's badge number was _____.

4. Steve McGarrett headed up the
   Honolulu-based unit known as "Hawaii _____."

5. "Kookie" parked cars next door to "_____ Sunset Strip."

6. Tod Stiles, Buz Murdock, and Linc Case all
    rode a Corvette along "Route _____.

7. Dick Clark hosted this show. It began as "The _____ .
   Pyramid" and, with inflation, was increased to "The
   _____ Pyramid."

8. It didn't run long, but Lance Kerwin starred
   in a series back in the 1970s originally entitled "James at _____ ."

9. It was a landmark show during the "Golden Age of Television"
   known as "Playhouse _____ ."

10. Hogan's heroes were held in Stalag _____ .

Total your answers here _____

Test Number 2:

This set of ten is much more difficult than the first set. How does it add
up for you? The correct total is 14,157, 266.

11. Until the scandals, it was a huge hit show
    in the 1950s hosted by Hal March.
    It was "The _____ Question."

12. He was played by Lee Majors, he was bionic, and he was known
    as "The _____ Dollar Man."

13. Archie and Edith Bunker lived at _____ Houser Street.

14. Martin Milner and Kent McCord starred in this long-running
    police drama known as "Adam _____ ."

15. On this gritty police show of the early sixties, the narrator always
    informed viewers that there were " _____ stories in the
    Naked City."

16. On "Get Smart," Don Adams was Agent _____ , and Barbara Feldon was Agent _____ .

17. On "Mission: Impossible," Jim Phelps got his instructions on a tape that would "self-destruct in _____ seconds."

18. These teenagers are coming of age in Beverly Hills, zip code _____ ."

19. Famous as an example of a really bad television show, "My Mother the Car" was built on the premise that Jerry Van Dyke's mother had been reincarnated into an automobile, a _____ Porter.

20. Lloyd Haines and Karen Valentine starred in this series about teachers who taught at Walt Whitman High. His homeroom number was "Room _____ ."

Total your answers here _____

Test Number 3:

This set will add up to 1,001,157.

21. Through his minion, Michael Anthony, eccentric billionaire John Beresford Tipton gave away this sum each week. What sum? _____

22. On "The Dating Game," how many bachelors or "bachelorettes" were behind the partition? _____

23. What was the most money you could win on
"What's My Line?" _____

24. At last count, Carla Tortelli was the mother of _____
children.

25. Barney Miller and his crew worked out of the _____
Precinct in New York City.

26. It's one of the "reality-based" shows, and its title is
"Rescue _____ ."

27. Jack Benny's perennial age was _____ .

28. Dan Rather hosts this magazine show entitled " _____
Hours."

29. This clone of "77 Sunset Strip" was titled
"Surfside _____ ."

30. It ran for six years in the fifties on the premise that
"Life Begins at _____ ."

Total your answers here _____

This test will be a little simpler, or at least the numbers will be smaller. Try this one. Your total should be 2,004.

31. Number of years "60 Minutes" has been on the air, as of 1994 _____

32. Another reality-based show on Fox, called "Code _____ "

33. As of 1994, the number of years "The Today Show" has been on the air _____

34. Number of kids in The Brady Bunch _____

35. Number of years Johnny Carson hosted "The Tonight Show" _____

36. The sign over the entrance to Cheers, says the bar was established in _____ .

37. Number of roommates Jack Tripper had _____

38. Number of bullets Barney Fife carried _____

39. Number of doors on "Let's Make a Deal" _____

40. Number of children born to Mike and Gloria _____

Total your answers here _____

By the numbers, year by year. Supply the year the following things were seen on television, then add up those numbers. If your answers are correct, your total will be 700.

41.   The year "I Love Lucy" premiered 19 _____

42.   The year "The Beverly Hillbillies" was first seen 19 _____

43.   The Iran hostage crisis gives us "Nightline" 19 _____

44. Carter/Ford debate, first since Nixon/Kennedy 19 _____

45. "All in the Family" debuts 19 _____

46. The last year cigarette ads were seen on TV 19 _____

47. "I Have a Dream" speech first broadcast 19 _____

48. Last year Walter Cronkite anchored evening news 19 _____

49. The year viewers saw men on the moon 19 _____

50. "Roots" makes TV history 19 _____

Total your answers here _____

Test Number 6:

Low numbers. They add up to 11.

51. Number of jobs held by Ozzie on
     "The Adventures of Ozzie and Harriet" _____

52. Number of children Murphy Brown has had _____

53. Number of children Bob and Emily had, multiplied
     by the number of children Bob and Joanna had _____

54. Number of guests on CNN's "Crossfire" _____

55. Number of barbers in Mayberry _____

56. Number of times John Wayne appeared on "Gunsmoke" _____

57. Number of presidential candidates who have played
     the saxophone on "The Arsenio Hall Show" _____

58. Number of debates between Dan Quayle and Lloyd
     Bentsen during the 1988 presidential campaign _____

59. Number of poets who have read at televised presidential _____
     inaugurations _____

60. Number of sitcom stars in Gerald McRaney's household _____

                    Total your answers here _____

Your total for this set of seven should be 2,070.

61. Number of children in the Munster family _____

62. Number of children in the Addams family _____

63. Number of passengers aboard the Minnow when it wrecked _____

64. Number of people who have hosted versions of "You Bet Your Life" _____

65. Number of years the original "Star Trek" ran before going into syndication _____

66. Number of children on "Eight Is Enough" _____

67. Address Johnny Depp starred at on "Jump Street" _____

68. Newsmagazine show hosted by Hugh Downs _____

69. Number of members of "The A-Team" _____

70. Number of children born to Sonny and Cher _____

Total your answers here _____

Test Number 8:

If you know all the answers in the following tests, the numbers will add up to 342.

71. Kate and Allie's children number how many? _____

72. Mary Beth Lacey had how many children? _____

73. Chris Cagney had how many children? _____

74. Number of people who occupy "contestant's row" at any one time on "The Price is Right" _____

75. The invisible wall that separates the actors from the audience has a number. Shows like "It's Gary Shandling's Show" broke through this wall. It's known as the _____ wall.

76. According to its title, Fred MacMurray had how many sons in this series? _____

77. Number of children in the Rob and Laura Petrie household _____

78. Though they seldom moderate anything in this shouting match, how many "moderators" are there on CNN's "Crossfire"? _____

79. Number of guests who appeared each night on Whoopi Goldberg's talk show _____

80. PBS children's science show: "___–___–___ Contact" _____

Total your answers here _____

If you have all the numbers correct in the upcoming test, your answers
will total 40.

81. There were this many "Monkees" _____

82. Number of Bunker grandchildren _____

83. Number of years "Cheers" was on the air, not counting
     reruns _____

84. As of 1992, Tony Danza had been a regular on how many
     sitcoms? _____

85. How many Golden Girls were in the regular cast of
     "Golden Girls?" _____

86. Number of times the Beatles appeared on "The Ed
     Sullivan Show" _____

87. Number of times Elvis Presley appeared on "The Ed
     Sullivan Show" _____

88. Number of actresses who played "Charlie's Angels" _____

89. Number of TV series on which Warren Beatty has been
     a regular _____

90. How many "Not Ready for Prime Time Players"
     when "Saturday Night Live" debuted? _____

Total your answers here _____

Test Number 10:

If you get all the numbers right in this test, the result will total 765.

91. President Clinton likes this show. On "American Gladiators," how many contestants compete each week? _____

92. Number of syllables in the Orkan word for "good-bye" _____

93. Televangelist Pat Robertson launched this show in 1976. It's called "The _____ Club"

94. In 1989, "Sesame Street" celebrated an anniversary. Which anniversary? _____

95. Number of writers who worked for WJM-TV News _____

96. Number of categories contestants choose from on "Jeopardy!" _____

97. Number of contestants who compete in the final round of Jeopardy!" _____

98. Number of millions needed by Oral Roberts to save him from being recalled by God in 1987 _____

99. Age of Doogie Howser when the series began _____

100. Counting the cartoon show called "The Oddball Couple," how many TV series have been fashioned from Neil Simon's *The Odd Couple?* _____

Total your answers here _____

1. The "M*A*S*H" unit was number **4077.**

2. The prefix used for nearly all fictional phone numbers on television is **555.**

3. Joe Friday's badge number was **714.**

4. Steve McGarrett headed up the Honolulu-based unit known as **"Hawaii Five-O."**

5. "Kookie" parked cars next door to **"77 Sunset Strip."**

6. Tod Stiles, Buz Murdock, and Linc Case all rode a Corvette along **"Route 66."**

7. Dick Clark hosted this show. It began as **"The $10,000 Pyramid"** and, with inflation, was increased to **"The $25,000 Pyramid."**

8. It didn't run long, but Lance Kerwin starred in a series back in the 1970s entitled **"James at 15."**

9. It was a landmark show during the "Golden Age of Television" known as **"Playhouse 90."**

10. Hogan's heroes were held in Stalag **13.**

Total . . . 40,657

Answers

Answers

11. Until the scandals, it was a huge hit show in the 1950s hosted by Hal March. It was **"The $64,000 Question."**

12. He was played by Lee Majors, he was bionic, and he was known as **"The $6,000,000 Dollar Man."**

13. Archie and Edith Bunker lived at **704 Houser Street.**

14. Martin Milner and Kent McCord starred in this long-running police drama known as **"Adam 12."**

15. On this gritty police show of the early sixties, the narrator always informed viewers that there were **"8,000,000** stories in the Naked City."

16. On "Get Smart," Don Adams was Agent **86,** and Barbara Feldon was Agent **99.**

17. On "Mission: Impossible," Jim Phelps got his instructions on a tape that would "self-destruct in **5 seconds."**

18. These teenagers are coming of age in Beverly Hills, zip code **90210.**

19. Famous as an example of a really bad television show, "My Mother the Car," was built on the premise that Jerry Van Dyke's mother had been reincarnated into an automobile, a **1928** Porter.

20. Lloyd Haines and Karen Valentine starred in this series about teachers who taught at Walt Whitman High. His homeroom number was **"Room 222."**

Total . . . **14,157,266**

Answers

21. Through his minion, Michael Anthony, eccentric billionaire John Beresford Tipton gave away this sum each week. What sum? **$1,000,000**

22. On "The Dating Game," how many bachelors or "bachelorettes" were behind the partition? **3**

23. What was the most money you could win on "What's My Line"? **$50**

24. At last count, Carla Tortelli was the mother of **8** children.

25. Barney Miller and his crew worked out of the **12th** Precinct in New York City.

26. It's one of the "reality-based" shows, and its title is **"Rescue 911."**

27. Jack Benny's perennial age was **39.**

28. Dan Rather hosts this magazine show entitled **"48 Hours."**

29. This clone of "77 Sunset Strip" was titled **"Surfside Six."**

30. It ran for six years in the fifties on the premise that **"Life Begins at 80."**

Total . . . 1,001,157

Answers

31. Number of years "60 Minutes" has been on the air, as of 1994 — **26**

32. Another reality-based show on Fox, called "Code — **3**"

33. As of 1994, the number of years "The Today Show" has been on the air— **42**

34. Number of kids in "The Brady Bunch" — **6**

35. Number of years Johnny Carson hosted "The Tonight Show" — **25**

36. On the sign over the entrance to Cheers, the year it says the bar was established in — **1895**

37. Number of roommates Jack Tripper had — **2**

38. Number of bullets Barney Fife carried — **1**

39. Number of doors on "Let's Make a Deal" — **3**

40. Number of children born to Mike and Gloria — **1**

Total . . . **2,004**

Test Number 5:

41. The year "I Love Lucy" premiered —19**51**

42. The year "The Beverly Hillbillies" was first seen — 19**62**

43. The Iran hostage crisis gives us "Nightline" —1980

44. Carter/Ford debate, first since Nixon/Kennedy —1976

45. "All in the Family" debuts —1971

46. The last year cigarette ads were seen on TV — 1970

47. "I Have a Dream" speech first broadcast —1963

48. Last year Walter Cronkite anchored evening news —1981

49. The year viewers saw men on the moon —1969

50. "Roots" makes TV history —1977

Total . . .700

Test Number 6:

51. Number of jobs held by Ozzie on "The Adventures of Ozzie and Harriet" — **0**

52. Number of children Murphy Brown has had — **1**

53. Number of children Bob and Emily had, multiplied by the number of children Bob and Joanna had — **0**

54. Number of guests on CNN's "Crossfire" — **2**

55. Number of barbers in Mayberry — **1**

56. Number of times John Wayne appeared on "Gunsmoke" — **1**

57. Number of presidential candidates who have played the saxophone on "The Arsenio Hall Show" — **1**

58. Number of debates between Dan Quayle and Lloyd Bentsen during the 1988 presidential campaign — **1**

59. Number of poets who have read at televised presidential inaugurations — **2**

60. Number of sitcom stars in Gerald McRaney's household — **2**

Total . . . **11**

Test Number 7:

61. Number of children in the Munster family — **1**

62. Number of children in the Addams family — **2**

63. Number of passengers aboard the Minnow when it wrecked — **7**

64. Number of people who have hosted versions of "You Bet Your Life" — **3**

65. Number of years the original "Star Trek" ran before going into syndication — **3**

66. Number of children on "Eight Is Enough" — **8**

67. Address Johnny Depp starred at on Jump Street — **21**

68. Newsmagazine show hosted by Hugh Downs — **"20/20"**

69. Number of members of "The A-Team" — **4**

70. Number of children born to Sonny and Cher — **1**

Total 2,070

Test Number 8:

71. Kate and Allie's children number how many? — **3**

72. Mary Beth Lacey had how many children? — **3**

73. Chris Cagney had how many children? — **0**

74. Number of people who occupy "contestant's row" at any one time on "The Price is Right" — **4**

75. The invisible wall that separates the actors from the audience has a number. Shows like "It's Gary Shandling's Show" broke through this wall. It's known as the ____ wall — **4th**

76. According to its title, Fred MacMurray had how many sons in this series? — **3**

77. Number of children in the Rob and Laura Petrie household — **1**

78. Though they seldom moderate anything in this shouting match, how many "moderators" are there on CNN's "Crossfire"? — **2**

79. Number of guests appearing each night on Whoopi Goldberg's talk show — **1**

80. PBS children's science show. "___-___-___ Contact" — **3-2-1**

Total . . .342

Test Number 9:

81. There were this many "Monkees" — **4**

82. Number of Bunker grandchildren — **1**

83. Number of years "Cheers" was on the air, not counting reruns — **11**

84. As of 1992, Tony Danza had been a regular on how many sitcoms? — **2**

85. How many Golden Girls were in the regular cast of "Golden Girls"? — **4**

86. Number of times the Beatles appeared on "The Ed Sullivan Show" — **2**

87. Number of times Elvis Presley appeared on "The Ed Sullivan Show" — **2**

88. Number of actresses who played "Charlie's Angels" — **6**

89. Number of TV series on which Warren Beatty has been a regular — **1**

90. How many "Not Ready for Prime Time Players" when "Saturday Night Live" debuted? — **7**

Total . . . **40**

Test Number 10:

91. President Clinton likes this show. On "American Gladiators," how many contestants compete each week? — **4**

92. Number of syllables in the Orkan word for "good-bye" — **4**

93. Televangelist Pat Robertson launched this show in 1976. It's called "The _____ Club" — **700**

94. In 1989, "Sesame Street" celebrated an anniversary. Which anniversary? — **20**

95. Number of writers who worked for WJM-TV News — **1**

96. Number of categories contestants choose from on "Jeopardy!" — **6**

97. Number of contestants who compete in the final round of "Jeopardy!" — **3**

98. Number of millions needed by Oral Roberts to save him from being recalled by God in 1987 — **8**

99. Age of Doogie Howser when the series began — **16**

100. Counting the cartoon show called "The Oddball Couple," how many TV series have been fashioned from Neil Simon's *The Odd Couple*? — **3**

Total . . . **765**

Answers

There are one hundred questions in this chapter. You already know how well you did if you added up the numbers as you went along. Were you able to make even one set add up to the correct total? If so, you did quite well. More than one set, and you're not only knowledgeable about television (even obscure things about television) but you're also good at math. If, by some wizardry, you managed to know everything on this test, then your total figure for the entire chapter should be **15,205,012**.

14

Cable-Ready?

"Fifty-seven channels, and nothin' on."
BRUCE SPRINGSTEEN

Ok, admit it: Cable was ready for you before you were ready for cable. Sure, you wanted more channels to choose from, but when you got them, you hardly knew where to turn in the bewildering array of choices. All of a sudden, the numbers on the remote no longer necessarily corresponded to the number of your favorite station. A whole bunch of channels didn't really go by numbers at all; they were known by letters—C-SPAN, TNN, A&E. Sometimes you looked back fondly on the days when it was all so simple—Channel 4, Channel 5, Channel 7. Now you had to speed through all the numbers on the remote, fearful that you were missing something really good, something absolutely essential, on one of those mysterious channels.

Of course, if you're addicted to television, you'll deny that there was ever a time when you were daunted by the array of channels. Not you, you'll say; you were practically born with a remote-control channel changer in your hand. You're the person other people come to when they want to know what number corresponds to The Disney Channel. You know the whole smorgasbord of "Nick at Nite," and you know just where to find it, plus how to shuttle away to catch snatches of stand-up comedy on VH-1 during the commercials.

But remember that little talk you got from the cable installer way back when? Remember the card he left telling you all the channels, and that somehow, through the magic of cable, your old over-the-air CBS station no longer came in on that same number? You may not need that card anymore, but there was a time.

For many, that time remains. For some reason, women and older people have a much greater difficulty growing accustomed to the array of choices offered through cable. This series of tests will determine if you're cable-ready or cable-impaired, and we'll start with the basics.

Test Number 1: **CHANNEL SURFING**

In the test below, identify the cable networks.

(Caution: Some of these offerings may not be available in all areas. If you don't have cable, this test will be largely meaningless to you.)

1. A&E is the _____ & _____ network.

2. LIF stands for _____.

3. TBS is the _____.

4. CNN is the _____.

5. In the listings, MAX is short for _____.

6. AMC stands for _____.

7. DISC is the listing for _____ .

8. TMC is_____ .

9. MTV stands for _____ .

10. NICK is short for_____ .

11. E! is for_____ .

12. HBO, the pioneer of much of this, stands for

    _____ .

13. BVO stands for _____ .

14. PLAY is the listing for _____ .

15. TNT stands for_____ .

16. SHO is how _____ is listed.

17. COM is the listing for _____ .

18. TNN is how _____
    is listed.

19. DIS is the listing for_____ .

20. ENC is the listing for_____ .

If you have cable, and if you call yourself a channel surfer, then surely
you knew the answers to most of those. Now, however, you face addi-
tional challenges. You have to know how to use what you know to find
what you want to see. That brings us to . . .

Let's say you want to catch "Crook and Chase." (That may seem unlikely, but this is a hypothetical kind of deal.) What network would you turn to? In the test that follows, your job is to identify the network on which you would find the following programs.

21. "Crook and Chase" is found on _____ .

22. "Mystery Science Theatre 3000" is found on _____ .

23. For "Larry King Live," you turn to _____ .

24. "Evening at the Improv" is found on _____ .

25. "Moneyline" is on _____ .

26. "Tales From the Crypt" is produced for _____ .

27. "The A List" is on _____ .

28. "Super Dave" is found most often on _____ .

29. "Crossfire" is on _____ .

30. Your best shot at catching a showing of *Casablanca* is on _____ .

31. "Short Attention Span Theatre" is on_____ .

32. If you're intent on seeing Ralph Emery, you'll have to tune in _____ .

33. Jesse Jackson has a talk show. It's on _____ .

34. "Lip Service" is a program you'll find on _____ .

35. "Dream On" is a series on _____ .

36. "The Capitol Gang" is found on _____ .

37. "Kids in the Hall" is found on _____ .

38. "Ren and Stimpy" can be seen on _____ .

39. "The Larry Sanders Show" is made for _____ .

40. "Fantasies" is a show on _____ .

By now, you've either given up, or you've become hopelessly smug. Too easy, you say? Well, try the next test, which takes you beyond merely knowing where to find a particular cable program; in this test, you'll have to know something about the content of these cable programs. (Yes, some of them do have a bit of content, if you look hard enough.)

Do you know the name of the guy who plays Larry Sanders? Do you know what cable channel brought us Larry Sanders? No? And you call yourself a couch potato!

Let's see if you know . . .

Test Number 3: **WHAT'S ON CABLE?**

41. He's one of the stars of "Dream On," but he used to be a Steed. Name him. _____

42. He is the host of "The A List," but he was once on a show for ABC with Jamie Lee Curtis. Name him. _____

43. Name the show. _____

Cable-Ready?   275

44. One of Frank Zappa's kids is a VJ for MTV. What's does VJ stand for? _____ .

45. Name one of Zappa's kids. _____

46. For that matter, name the band Zappa fronted back in the sixties and seventies. _____

47. Pauly Shore gave us the movie *Encino Man*. What cable network gave us Pauly Shore? _____

48. Dick Van Dyke is a spokesman for a cable channel that he says is "preserving our television heritage." What that means is a lot of sitcom reruns. What cable channel is this? _____

49. "Inside the Comedy Mind" is an interview show. Who is the host? _____

50. These two newspaper columnists have a political commentary show on CNN. One is Robert ("Bob," for short); the other is Rowland. The show goes by their last names, however. They are? And the show is? " _____ and _____ ."

51. He's an anchorman for CNN, the one who asked Michael Dukakis how he'd feel if Kitty Dukakis were raped and murdered. Name him. _____

52. This is the guy who gives those great introductions to old movies on the American Movie Channel. If you've seen him, you've probably liked him. If you liked him, you'll remember his name. _____

53. "Showbiz Today" is CNN's answer to "Entertainment Tonight". The hostesses are Bela _____ and Lauren _____ .

54. This is an early-morning children's fitness show called "Mousercise." Even if you don't have kids, you probably know it can be found on The _____ Channel.

55. It's on ESN; it's an adult exercise show; it's called "Body by _____."

56. Personally, I don't like this guy, but maybe you do. He hosts a show on Comedy Central called "Comics Only." Who's he? _____

57. "Ren and Stimpy" achieved instant cult status. In this cartoon series, Ren is a _____ and Stimpy is a _____ .

58. "Crossfire" features, "on the right, _____ , and from the left _____."

59. Name the cable channel where you'd be most likely to find reruns of "Mr. Ed." _____

60. "Sonya Live!" is an interview show on _____ .

61. Delta Burke starred in this HBO series when it debuted in 1984. She played the owner of a football team called the California Bulls. Its title? _____

62. It was produced for Showtime and it pioneered the portrayal of a major homosexual character. It starred Robert Walden. Can you name that long-running series? _____

63. He's a correspondent for CNN. His first name is Wolf; his last name is _____ .

64. It's on the USA network now, but it began as a series on HBO in 1983. Nicholas Campbell and Page Fletcher have both held the title role. That title role is "The _____ ."

65. MTV apparently threatened western civilization when they gave us two animated adolescent morons named _____ and _____ .

1. A&E is the **Arts & Entertainment** network.

2. LIF stands for **Lifetime**.

3. TBS is the **Turner Broadcasting System**.

4. CNN is the **Cable News Network**.

5. In the listings, MAX is short for **Cinemax**.

6. AMC stands for **The American Movie Channel**.

7. DISC is the listing for **The Discovery Channel**.

8. TMC is **The Movie Channel**.

9. MTV stands for **Music Television**.

10. NICK is short for **Nickelodeon**.

11. E! is for **Entertainment!**

12. HBO, the pioneer of much of this, stands for **Home Box Office**.

13. BVO stands for **Bravo**.

14. PLAY is the listing for **The Playboy Channel**.

15. TNT stands for **Turner Network Television**.

16. SHO is how **Showtime** is listed.

17. COM is the listing for **Comedy Central**.

18. TNN is how **The Nashville Network** is listed.

19. DIS is the listing for **The Disney Channel**.

Answers

20. ENC is the listing for **Encore**.

Test Number 2: **PROGRAM PROBE**

21. "Crook and Chase" is found on **The Nashville Network**.

22. "Mystery Science Theatre 3000" is found on **Comedy Central**.

23. For "Larry King Live" you turn to **Cable News Network**.

24. "Evening at the Improv" is found on **Arts & Entertainment**.

25. "Moneyline" is on **Cable News Network**.

26. "Tales From the Crypt" is produced for **Home Box Office**.

27. "The A List" is on **Comedy Central**.

28. Super Dave is found most often on **Showtime**.

29. "Crossfire" is on **Cable News Network**.

30. Your best shot at catching a showing of *Casablanca* is on **The American Movie Channel**.

31. "Short Attention Span Theatre" is on **Comedy Central**.

32. If you're intent on seeing Ralph Emery, you'll have to tune in **The Nashville Network**.

33. Jesse Jackson has a talk show. It's on **Cable News Network**.

34. "Lip Service" is a program you'll find on **Music Television**.

35. "Dream On" is a series on **Home Box Office**.

Answers

36. "The Capital Gang" is found on **Cable News Network**.

37. "Kids in the Hall" is found on **Comedy Central**.

38. "Ren and Stimpy" can be seen on **Nickelodeon**.

39. "The Larry Sanders Show" is made for **Home Box Office**.

40. "Fantasies" is a show on **The Playboy Channel**.

Test Number 3: **WHAT'S ON CABLE?**

41. **Patrick McNee** is one of the stars of "Dream On." He used to play John Steed on "The Avengers."

42. He is the host of "The A List," but **Richard Lewis** was once on a show for ABC with Jamie Lee Curtis.

43. The name of the show was **"Anything But Love."**

44. VJ stands for **video jockey**.

45. Zappa's kids' names are **Dweezil** and **Moon Unit**.

46. Zappa fronted the **Mothers of Invention** back in the sixties and seventies.

47. Pauly Shore was given to us by **Music Televison**.

Cable-Ready?

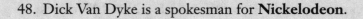

Answers

48. Dick Van Dyke is a spokesman for **Nickelodeon**.

49. **Alan King** is the host of "Inside the Comedy Mind."

50. Rowland is **Evans** and Robert is **Novak** and the show is called **"Evans and Novak."**

51. **Bernard Shaw** is the CNN newscaster who asked Michael Dukakis how he'd feel if Kitty Dukakis were raped and murdered.

52. **Bob Dorian** is the likeable guy who introduces the movies on AMC.

53. "Showbiz Today" is hosted by Bela **Shaw** and Lauren **Sydney**.

54. The early-morning children's fitness show called "Mousercise" is on The **Disney** Channel.

55. The adult exercise show on ESN is "Body by **Jake**."

56. **Paul Provenza** hosts "Comics Only."

57. Ren is a **Chihuahua** and Stimpy is an overweight **cat**.

58. "Crossfire" features, "on the right, **Pat Buchanan** or **John Sununu**, and from the left **Michael Kinsley**."

59. Reruns of "Mr. Ed" can be seen on **Nickelodeon**.

60. "Sonya Live!" is an interview show on **Cable News Network**.

61. Delta Burke was the owner of a football team called the California Bulls on **"1st & 10."**

62. **"Brothers"** pioneered the portrayal of a major homosexual character.

63. Wolf **Blitzer** is a correspondent for CNN.

64. Nicholas Campbell and Page Fletcher have both played "The **Hitchhiker.**"

65. MTV's animated adolescent morons are **Beavis** and **Butthead.**

It's anticipated that there will soon be as many as five hundred cable channels available to viewers. Aren't you glad you didn't have to take a test on all that?

If cable hasn't reached you yet, then this chapter is a lost cause, although many of these people and things are reported on in the print media and on network television. Even if you don't get cable, I'll bet you knew answers to at least ten of the sixty-five questions in this test.

Scoring

45–65 Correct: You are, indeed, cable-ready.

25–44 Correct: Slow down with that remote.

0–24 Correct: Not cable-ready.

15

Super Trivia

"I know what I know, if you know what I mean."
EDIE BRICKELL AND THE NEW BOHEMIANS

This chapter is a compendium of things. There are no categories; it comes to you as television does: all mixed up, fragmented, disordered. But, if you've watched much television, you'll know some of this—maybe even more than some.

It all depends on what you've seen, and what you remember of what you've seen. Though I can't speak for all viewers, I find that what adheres to my memory tends to be rather random. By any measure, however, the questions in this next test are pretty obscure. The test that follows may be the most challenging in this book. If you do well on it, then you have surely been watching too much television, reading too much about television—and you've got a terrific memory. Did Sam and

Diane get together on the last episode of "Cheers"? What was Maggie Simpson's first word, and what actress provided that cartoon character with a voice? It may be trivia, but it's omnipresent in the culture, and it can be fun to know it, and know that you know it.

Try these.

1. On "Cheers," what is Woody's middle name? _____

2. What is Michael J. Fox's real middle initial? _____

3. The last name of the character played by Andy Kaufman on "Taxi" was_____ .

4. The name of the character played by Robert Culp on "Trackdown," his first television series, was _____ .

5. College attended by Reverend Jim Ignatowski?_____

6. The word Dr. Johnny Fever said on the air that got him fired from his job in California? _____

7. On the "60 Minutes" segment called "Point/Counterpoint" (later satirized on "Saturday Night Live" and copied for a Ramada Inn commercial), he was _____ and she was _____ .

8. The name of the bartender in Miss Kitty's saloon? _____ (If you can't remember his name, I'll bet you remember what he looked like.)

9. Where did Maxwell Smart keep his phone? _____

10. During his presidency, Ronald Reagan said this was his favorite television show. What was it? _____

11. On "The Dukes of Hazzard," Luke and Bo had a car, and the car had a name. What name? _____

12. Who hosted "The $1.98 Beauty Show"? _____

13. Who played the corpse—his face was never seen on screen—in the movie *The Big Chill*. (Some critics thought it was a stretch for this actor.) _____

14. What is written on the two nuclear warheads in Stanley Kubrick's classic apocalyptic film *Dr. Strangelove, Or, How I Learned to Stop Worrying and Love the Bomb*? _____
    and _____

15. The guy who videotaped the Rodney King beating sold it to a Los Angeles television station.
    How much did he sell it for? _____

16. Name either or both of Beaver Cleaver's teachers.
    Miss _____
    and Miss _____

17. Alex P. Keaton kept a portrait of an American president on the wall. Which president? _____
    And can you name Alex P. Keaton's
    favorite television show? _____

18. This martial arts hero got his start playing Kato on "The Green Hornet," a mid-sixties sequel to the popular radio show of the same name. Name that martial arts hero. _____

19. And name his son, recently killed on the set of his own martial arts movie. _____

20. She would go on to movie stardom, but her 1977 TV debut in a cop show called "Dog and Cat" sank like a stone, lasting less than

six weeks. When she got rich, she bought an entire town in her home state of Georgia. Name her. _____

21. He appeared on nearly fifty television shows, but "Man With a Camera" was the only series he starred in. His real name is Charles Buchinsky.
What name do we know him by? _____

22. On "Cheers," Lilith's maiden name? _____

23. He's the son of a famous radio comic; he was "the guy under the seats" on "Late Night With David Letterman." He had his own show called "Get a Life." He is _____ .

24. Ralph Kramden and Ed Norton belonged to this lodge.
_____

25. He walked off his show because the network wouldn't let him say "W.C." Who was he and what does "W.C." stand for?
_____

26. He walked off his newscast and presidential candidate George Bush later chided him for it.
Name the newsman. _____

27. Comedians "die" on television all the time, but this talk show host had a guest who literally died on the air.
Name the host._____

28. Lou Grant's wife: her first name, please. _____

29. That famous theme music for "Alfred Hitchcock Presents"?
You can probably hum a few bars, but I bet you can't name it.
_____

30. Ironically, this pop icon did a public service advertisement for

highway safety shortly before dying in an early morning car accident in California. Name him. _____

31. Alan Brady's brother-in-law and producer? _____

32. Name of Dick Loudon's bed-and-breakfast place? _____

33. The kind of car the guys drove on "Route 66." _____

34. The name of the cook on "Rawhide"? _____

35. That commercial where the guy comes to borrow coffee, and begins to fall for the pretty neighbor, and then it goes on like a soap opera where we are all supposed to wonder whether the two of them ever get together: What brand of coffee was this mini-serial made to advertise?_____

36. Who said this: "I'm envious of Murphy Brown. At least she is guaranteed to come back next fall."_____

37. A British butler got stranded in Mayberry. He had once served in the Cold Stream Guards. Gomer, of course, couldn't get it right. He thought the man had served in the _____ Guards.

38. A granddaughter of an American literary legend had her own show. Name her and name the show. _____

39. What was Lucy Ricardo's maiden name? _____

40. What was Rhoda Morgenstern's married name?_____

41. Mary Tyler Moore returned to the land of sitcoms in 1985 with a show that lasted half a season.
What was the name of that show?_____

42. The voice of Mr. Ed was provided by a star of 1940s B westerns. His name was _____.

43. Back in 1979, before he made a name for himself, this actor played Lance White on "The Rockford Files." He was also a poster boy for Camel cigarettes.
Who's he? _____

44. On "Bonanza," David Canary played the recurring role of Candy, but soap opera fans now know him as both _____ and _____ on "_____."

45. Before he was the Lone Ranger, he was one of six Texas Rangers. The rest of them were ambushed and wiped out by a gang of bad guys. The name of the leader of that gang was _____ .

46. What's the name of the "tool girl" on "Tool Time"? _____

47. Johnny Carson had his most famous feud with a comedienne who often filled in for him. Apparently, he's still not talking to her. Who's she? _____

48. Who wrote the Clinton/Gore theme song that Hillary and Tipper danced to at the Democratic Convention? _____

49. Who conducted the "60 Minutes" interview with Woody Allen in which Woody displayed the skewered Valentine Mia Farrow had sent him? _____

50. Andy Rooney was once suspended from "60 Minutes." Do you remember why? _____

51. This was the only series (so far) written, produced, and directed by Steve Martin. It lasted a few months back in 1986, and it starred Harvey Korman and Valerie Perrine. Bet you never heard of it. _____

52. On "Let's Make a Deal," when you picked the door with the worthless stuff behind it, that was called a _____ .

53. Markie Post had two TV series before "Hearts Afire." One of them was "Night Court."
Can you name the other? _____

54. Bob Barker often signs off "The Price Is Right" by urging viewers to do something regarding animals.
He urges us to _____ .

55. On cable-ready television screens, you will sometimes see the letters *SAP*. What do those letters stand for?_____

56. In "The Wild, Wild West," agent James West had a nemesis, played by dwarf actor Michael Dunn.
Name that nemesis._____

57. (Easier one.) The name of the paper
Clark Kent worked for was _____ .

58. Of the following game shows, which *was never* hosted by Bill Cullen: "Name That Tune," "Down You Go," "The Price Is Right," "Let's Make a Deal," "To Tell the Truth," "The $25,000 Pyramid," "The Joker's Wild"?_____

59. "Batman," 1966–68. Which of the following was not one of his archenemies? a. The Riddler b. The Joker c. Egghead
d. Catwoman e. Pruneface f. The Penguin _____

60. According to the television series that bore his name, Bat Masterson's weapon of choice was_____ .

61. Be a Hall monitor: Match the Hall to his or her show.

    a. Huntz Hall _____   1. "Ramar of the Jungle"

b. Monty Hall _____ 2. "The Arsenio Hall Show"

c. Deidre Hall _____ 3. "Days of Our Lives"

d. Jon Hall _____ 4. "Saturday Night Live"

e. Anthony Michael Hall _____ 5. "Let's Make a Deal"

f. Arsenio Hall _____ 6. "The Chicago Teddy Bears"

62. Of the following people, which one played Tarzan in the television series of the same name?
   a. Lex Barker b. Edgar Rice Burroughs c. Ron Ely
   d. Johnny Weissmuller _____

63. "Gidget" gadget: The series ran in the mid-sixties.
   a. Who played Gidget?_____
   b. (Really hard one.) Who appeared as
      Gidget's friend Norman Durfner?_____
   c. (Almost as hard.) What high school
      did Gidget and Norman attend?_____

64. Two cartoon shows were spun off from "Gilligan's Island." (Can you believe that?) Name either of them. _____

65. It was one of several series McLean Stevenson starred in after he left "M*A*S*H." He played a radio talk show host, but he hasn't been heard from much since this series flopped in 1980. Name the series. _____

66. One of the biggest flops in television history was a monster two-hour variety/talk show that came and went in 1963. ABC invested $16 million in initial production money. The show was heavily promoted, but it bombed. It starred half of a famous comedy team of the 1950s. If you can name him, you've named the show.

_____

67. Having made it big in two Clint Eastwood movies, this orangutan star tried to capitalize on his fame by playing a supersmart talking simian who advised the government on nuclear policy. It was supposed to be *the* hit series of 1983, but viewers wouldn't monkey with it.
Name the series. _____

68. Didn't they know we didn't like this guy, with his arrogance and his toupee? Apparently not; ABC gave him a show called "Saturday Night Live With _____ " that premiered just a few weeks before the "real" "Saturday Night Live." Name him, and you'll tell it like it is regarding this famous talking head.

69. Once he was Lenny on "Laverne and Shirley," but he rose to mock rock "stardom" as David St. Hubbins of the ersatz heavy metal band known as_____ .

70. The highest-rated single program of the 1984–85 season was titled *The Burning Bed*. It marked a turn in the career of this actress, who had formerly been considered incapable of such a serious, nonglamorous role. Name her. _____

71. *Izzy and Moe* was a made-for-TV movie that reunited two major stars. Izzy and Moe were played by _____ and _____ .

72. Name all three founding hosts of HBO's first "Comic Relief" in 1986. _____ , _____ , and _____ .

73. There were two TV movies about this event—*Raid on Entebbe* and *Victory at Entebbe*.
a. Where is Entebbe? _____
b. Who was the leader of this country at the time of the raid?
_____

74. Steven Spielberg directed this famous made-for-TV movie about a hapless motorist harassed by a big truck. It starred Dennis Weaver. Name the movie._____

75. He was once a character named Gopher on "The Love Boat," but now he's a U.S. representative. What a country! Name this congressman from Iowa. _____

76. Not a hard question, if you're over forty. Name Liza (with a *Z*) Minnelli's mother. _____

77. "A Man and His Music: Parts 1 and 2": two TV specials from the 1960s. What man?_____

78. *Helter Skelter*, a four-hour TV movie: What and who was it about?_____

79. It was among her last TV appearances. In 1985, she played a homeless woman in a made-for-TV movie called *Stone Pillow*. Name her. _____

80. His only two TV series were "East Side/West Side" (1963–64) and "Mr. President" (1987–88). Name him. _____

81. *Out on a Limb*: her book, her made-for-TV movie. In this life, she is _____ .

82. Al Capone's vault. What could be in there? Remember the hype. This guy hosted the suspense. Who's he?_____

83. Big news coverage of this 1987 event—a baby trapped down a well in Texas. Do you remember the baby's name?_____

84. In a rare TV cameo, he played racist George Lincoln Rockwell in the "Roots" sequel entitled "The Next Generations."_____

85. Roy Rogers's horse was named Trigger. What was the name of Dale Evans's horse?_____
And what was the name of the jeep on the Rogers' ranch?

_____ .

86. "Sanford and Son" was adapted from a British TV series called "_____ and Son."

87. "All in the Family" was adapted from a British TV series called

_____ .

88. Fill in the blanks:

"Boy, the way _____ played,

Songs that made the _____ ,

Guys like us, we _____ .

Those _____ ."

89. The coronation of Queen Elizabeth II was seen by viewers all over the globe. What year was that? _____

90. The Army/McCarthy hearings: What year were they held ?

_____

91. The Watergate hearings: Who presided over them? _____

92. The Clarence Thomas confirmation hearings:
Who chaired the committee? _____

93. "We build excitement": advertising slogan.
Who "built excitement"? _____

94. In an emotional farewell, she gave her replacement an alarm clock. Name them both. _____ and

_____

95. He's a sportscaster who is overly fond of drawing crude play diagrams, and he's also a spokesman for Ace Hardware.
He is _____.

96. Animated animal spin-off from "The Cabbage Patch Kids," featuring Holly and Brattina? _____

97. a. Jack Benny's theme song? _____
    b. Bob Hope's theme song? _____

98. What state gave us Jane Pauley,
    David Letterman, and Hoagy Carmichael? _____

99. When he appeared on a talk show in the 1960s wearing a shirt made out of the American flag, censors blocked out the shirt.
Who was he? _____

100. Since leaving "Diff'rent Strokes," this actor keeps getting busted for drug-related infractions. He is _____.

Answers

1. Woody's middle name is **Tiberius**.

2. Michael J. Fox's real middle initial is **A**.

3. Andy Kaufman played the character Latka **Gravas**.

4. Robert Culp was **Hoby Gilman** in the 1950s western "Trackdown."

5. Reverend Jim Ignatowski went to **Harvard**.

6. The word Dr. Johnny Fever said on the air that got him fired was **"booger."**

7. **James Kilpatrick** was the "he" and **Shana Alexander** was the "she" on "Point/Counterpoint."

8. **Sam** was the bartender in Miss Kitty's saloon.

9. Maxwell Smart kept his phone in his **shoe**.

10. Ronald Reagan said **"Family Ties"** was his favorite television show.

11. Luke and Bo called their car **General Lee**.

12. **Rip Taylor** hosted this tacky 1970s game show.

13. **Kevin Costner** played the corpse in _The Big Chill_.

14. The two nuclear warheads in _Dr. Strangelove: Or, How I Learned to Stop Worrying and Love the Bomb_ bear the phrases **"Hi There"** and **"Dear John."**

15. The Rodney King tape initially was sold to a Los Angeles television station for **$500**.

16. Beaver Cleaver's teachers were Miss **Landers** and Miss **Canfield**.

17. Alex P. Keaton kept a portrait of **Ronald Reagan** on his wall. Alex P. Keaton's favorite television show was **"Wall Street Week."**

18. **Bruce Lee** got his start on "The Green Hornet."

19. His son's name is **Brandon Lee**.

20. **Kim Basinger** made her TV debut in "Dog and Cat."

21. Charles Buchinsky is also known as **Charles Bronson**.

22. Lilith's maiden name is **Sternin**.

23. **Chris Elliott**, son of Bob Elliott, was "the guy under the seats."

24. Ralph Kramden and Ed Norton were members of the **Raccoon Lodge**.

25. **Jack Paar** walked off his show because the network wouldn't let him say "W.C.," which stands for **water closet**, a British locution for bathroom.

26. **Dan Rather** walked off "The CBS Evening News" in September 1987 because he was irked that the newscast was to be delayed by the U.S. Open tennis tournament.

27. **Dick Cavett** was the host when his guest, a fitness expert died.

28. Lou Grant's wife was named **Edie**.

Answers

Answers

29. The theme music for "Alfred Hitchcock Presents" was **"The Funeral March of a Marionette"** by Charles Gounod.

30. **James Dean** did a public service advertisement for highway safety shortly before he died in a car accident.

31. Alan Brady's brother-in-law and producer was **Mel Cooley**.

32. The name of Dick's bed-and-breakfast place was the **Stratford Inn**.

33. Tod and Buz drove a 1960 **Corvette** along "Route 66."

34. **Wishbone**, played by Paul Brinegar, was the cook on "Rawhide."

35. **Taster's Choice** is the coffee that keeps us guessing.

36. Former vice president **Dan Quayle** expressed envy of Murphy Brown.

37. Gomer thought the man had served in the **Cold Cream** Guards.

38. Ernest Hemingway's granddaughter **Mariel Hemingway** starred in the show **"Civil Wars."**

39. Lucy's maiden name was **MacGillicuddy**.

40. Rhoda's married name was **Gerard**.

41. Mary Tyler Moore's short-lived 1985 sitcom was called **"Mary."**

42. The voice of Mr. Ed was provided by **Rocky Lane**.

43. **Tom Selleck** played Lance White on "The Rockford Files" and was a Camel cigarette poster boy.

44. Soap opera fans know David Canary as **Adam** and **Stewart Chandler** on **"All My Children."**

45. **Butch Cavendish** and his Hole in the Wall gang ambushed the group of Texas Rangers of which the Lone Ranger was a part.

46. **Lisa** is the "tool girl" on "Tool Time."

47. Johnny Carson and **Joan Rivers** haven't been getting along well.

48. The Clinton/Gore theme song, "Don't Stop Thinking About Tomorrow," was written and performed by **Fleetwood Mac.**

49. **Steve Kroft** interviewed Woody.

50. Andy Rooney was **publicly accused of having made ethnic slurs against a colleague.**

51. Steve Martin's failed series was called **"Leo and Liz in Beverly Hills."**

52. The door with the worthless stuff behind it was called a **zonk.**

53. Markie Post's other earlier series was **"The Fall Guy."**

54. Bob Barker, a stong spokesman for animal rights, often signs off "The Price Is Right" by urging us to **control the pet population by having our pets spayed or neutered.**

55. The letters *SAP* stand for **Second Audio Program.**

56. Agent James West's nemesis was **Dr. Miguelito Loveless.**

57. Clark Kent worked for the **Daily Planet.**

58. Perennial game show host Bill Cullen never hosted **"Let's Make a Deal."**

59. "Batman," 1966–68: **(e) Pruneface** was not one of his archenemies.

60. Bat Masterson's weapon of choice was **his cane**.

61. a. Huntz Hall: **(6) "The Chicago Teddy Bears"**

b. Monty Hall: **(5) "Let's Make a Deal"**

c. Deidre Hall: **(3) "Days of Our Lives"**

d. Jon Hall: **(1) "Ramar of the Jungle"**

e. Anthony Michael Hall: **(4) "Saturday Night Live"**

f. Arsenio Hall: **(2) "The Arsenio Hall Show"**

62. **(c) Ron Ely** played Tarzan in the television series.

63. a. **Sally Field** played Gidget in the 1960s series.

b. **Richard Dreyfuss** appeared as Gidget's friend Norman.

c. Gidget and Norman attended **Westside High**.

64. **"The New Adventures of Gilligan"** and **"Gilligan's Planet"** were the two cartoon shows spun off from "Gilligan's Island."

65. McLean Stevenson played Larry Alder, a Portland, Oregon, talk show host on the series **"Hello, Larry."**

66. **Jerry Lewis** hosted the 1963 flop "The Jerry Lewis Show."

67. The series that starred Clint Eastwood's orangutan pal, C. J., was called **"Mr. Smith."**

68. "Saturday Night Live With **Howard Cosell**" was the name of this clinker.

69. Lenny (actor Michael McKean) became David St. Hubbins of the

ersatz heavy metal band known as **Spinal Tap**.

70. **Farrah Fawcett** starred in *The Burning Bed*.

71. *Izzy and Moe* reunited **Jackie Gleason** and **Art Carney**.

72. The three founding hosts of HBO's first "Comic Relief" in 1986 were **Whoopi Goldberg**, **Robin Williams**, and **Billy Crystal**.

73. a. Entebbe is in **Uganda**.
    b. **Idi Amin** was its leader at the time of the raid.

74. Steven Spielberg directed *Duel*, the movie about a hapless motorist harassed by a big truck.

75. Representative **Fred Grandy** played Gopher on "The Love Boat."

76. Liza's mother was **Judy Garland**.

77. "A Man and His Music: Parts 1 and 2" starred **Frank Sinatra**.

78. *Helter Skelter* was about **Charles Manson and the Tate/LaBianca murders**.

79. **Lucille Ball** played a homeless woman in Stone Pillow.

80. **George C. Scott** starred in "East Side/West Side" and "Mr. President."

81. *Out on a Limb*: **Shirley MacLaine**

82. Al Capone's vault: **Geraldo Rivera**

83. The baby trapped down a well in Texas was **Jessica McClure**.

84. **Marlon Brando** played George Lincoln Rockwell in "The Next Generations."

85. Dale's horse was **Buttermilk** and the jeep was called **Nellybelle**.

86. "Sanford and Son" was adapted from the British series called **"Steptoe** and Son."

87. "All in the Family" was adapted from a British TV series called **"Till Death Do Us Part."**

88. Fill in the blanks:
    "Boy, the way **Glenn Miller** played,

    Songs that made the **hit parade**,

    Guys like us, we **had it made**.

    Those **were the days**."

89. The coronation of Queen Elizabeth II was in **1953**.

90. The Army/McCarthy hearings were in **1954**.

91. **Senator Sam Ervin** presided over the Watergate hearings.

92. **Senator Joe Biden** chaired the Clarence Thomas confirmation hearings.

93. **Pontiac** claimed to "build excitement."

94. **Jane Pauley** gave an alarm clock to **Deborah Norville**.

95. **John Madden** is the diagramming sportscaster.

96. The animated animal spin-off featuring Holly and Brattina was **"Pound Puppies."**

97. a. Jack Benny's theme song: **"Love in Bloom"**
    b. Bob Hope's theme song: **"Thanks for the Memory"**

98. Jane Pauley, David Letterman, and Hoagy Carmichael all hailed from **Indiana**.

99. **Abbie Hoffman** had his shirt censored.

100. **Todd Bridges** keeps getting in trouble with the law.

Answers

What's obscure, and what's not obscure? That depends on what you know. There is much in this chapter that *I* think is obscure, but for real TV trivia buffs, this might have been a breeze. Whether or not you did well, I hope you found some interesting things among these one hundred questions.

Scoring

90–100 Correct: A blue-ribbon TV trivia expert.

70–89 Correct: A solid score.

40–69 Correct: Still a very good score for this test.

20–39 Correct: Still no failure here.

0–19 Correct: Now we're talking failure.

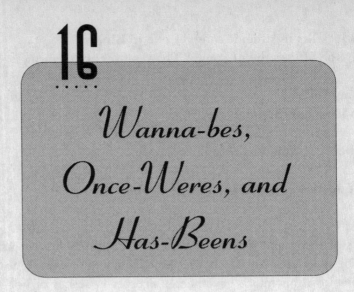

16

Wanna-bes, Once-Weres, and Has-Beens

"Today's audience knows more about what's on television than what's in life."

LARRY GELBART

When David Letterman left NBC for CBS, it was front-page news throughout the country. Some TV stations broke into regular programming with bulletins about it. The $16 million contract was part of the story, of course, but more and more, the personalities and the business of show business are big news. As a culture, we take this business seriously, and we form strong opinions about the people who are the objects of so much of our attention. This chapter focuses on some of those opinions that have been created—either by the stars themselves or by the media that reports on them. You'll find some personal bias in this chapter, and you may not agree with it all, but I hope the clues in the questions will lead you to the correct answers, even when you disagree.

Show business is a cruel business, rather like life itself. There is the time when fortunes are on the rise, and the time when they are on the wane. Beauty blossoms, then fades.

Certainly part of the obsession we have with stardom and celebrity is connected with the fact that careers in showbiz are public displays of the arc of our own lives. It's a cliché to say that movie and TV stars act out our dreams, but just as significantly, they act out our nightmares, too, our fear of falling. And it is an all-too-human element of our natures that we take some guilty comfort from the decline and fall of people we once admired, and perhaps felt inferior to. Despite our disclaimers to the contrary, we read the tabloids to see the decline of people who once occupied the heights. We make icons of people like ourselves, but we're reassured when we find them fashioned of the same clay we ourselves are fashioned from. As beautiful and talented as they may be, they still divorce, still have money worries, still make bad decisions, and, most of all, just like the rest of us, they age.

We pay these people such outrageous sums of money because they act out our lives for us, not only on the screen, but in the press. We cheer them on when they are rising, then swell ourselves with corrosive pity for them when they are on the decline. We thrill when one of them manages a comeback, because that speaks a parable of hope for our own lives. Graciously, we applaud them on the awards shows when they are brought back doddering from the brink of the grave to receive lifetime achievement awards, or other honors.

Not exactly the most upbeat premise for a TV trivia test, but these elements are vital to the complicated relationship we develop with these people we know so well, yet really don't know at all. Perhaps you are one of the world's better-adjusted souls who remains unmindful (and unenvious) of the success of others; perhaps you are among those noble people who would never take even the most secretive pleasure in a celebrity's failures. If so, this is a test you'll want to pass over.

However, if you count yourself in with the general run of humanity, you'll want to see if you remember these high and low lights from some famous careers.

I don't expect anyone to do very well on the upcoming test. It has to do with the often obscure and brief early work of people who became

Wanna-bes, Once-Weres, and Has-Beens

much more famous later on. Many actors and actresses who went on to become major stars had inauspicious beginnings on short-lived television series. We took little note of them at the time, but they were beginning to make their marks, beginning to win us over.

When it comes to major stars on television, the system seems to work in such a way that we catch them either on their way up or on their way down. Hungry future stars will turn up in unexpected places, playing small parts or playing leads in unsuccessful sitcoms. Then, just a few years later, they are commanding astronomical salaries, appearing in movie blockbusters, and turning up on television only long enough to promote their movies on the most prestigious of the talk shows, or doing brief filmed interviews with "Entertainment Tonight," the video version of *Variety* for those of us who do not work in the entertainment business. Then, after these stars have reached their ascendancy, the pull of age and gravity bring them back within the range of television, where, once again, we find them with their own sitcom or cop show. When the arc of the career is complete, these stars—their luster rapidly dimming—can be seen sailing into the sunset on "The Love Boat," or on "Murder, She Wrote," or as some panelist on a syndicated game show.

Once, when I was an adolescent, I remember noting a particular actor who had once been "big." He was taking roles that would have once been far below his stature. I had complicated feelings about this. First, there was a vague fear; what was happening to him was a model of what could and did happen to "ordinary" people—a progression toward success, followed by the inevitable decline. This, I would later learn, was the stuff of classic drama, of tragedy even. But I also had the luxury of feeling pity for a man who, even in decline, could make more money doing a single commercial than my father would make in ten years of very hard work. It's no exaggeration to say that our relationship with these celebrities is more complicated than we know, and like other more immediate relationships, it can tell us more about our individual selves than we will ever really know about the object of our fascination.

Since we track showbiz careers with more attention than we do any other kinds of careers (with the possible exception of a few politicians), watching the rise and fall of entertainment people becomes our way of assessing the meanings of success and failure. In these public lives, we

The Ultimate Test of TV TRIVIA

monitor our own sense of what it means to get ahead, or what it feels like to fall behind. We project onto these highly visible people all our fears and hopes and dreams. Within the space of a few years, we can revere them, envy them, hate them, and pity them. In fact, we may have more interest in watching the rise and fall of these celebrities than we do in watching their performances.

Discovering them early is the best part. If we take an interest, and if we like them, our best feelings are elicited. We wish them well, cheer them on, are gratified by their incremental successes. In them, we see our own struggles rewarded, see the dream of making it played out, and are reassured that lightning can still strike, that hurdles can be overcome by talent, luck, and good breaks. Virtues will be rewarded; talent or ability will be recognized. We want very much to believe that, and the entire entertainment industry provides us with that affirmation as, each year, it brings us the newest stars, people who have gone from K mart to Rodeo Drive in a single bound. This story, even more than the dramas these actors and actresses appear in, fuels our hopes. We live their successes with them.

Test Number 1: **MOVIN' ON UP**

So, this little test is about that stage of celebrity careers when our relationship with them is sweetest and most benign, before we've begun to envy them their success, while we are still vicariously sharing the pleasure of their rise. Were you a witness to the birth of any of these stars? Match the star to the series or miniseries that helped bring him or her to our attention.

1. Debra Winger _____

2. Michael Keaton _____

3. Kim Basinger _____

a. "Rich Man, Poor Man"

b. "Renegades"

c. "Richard Diamond, Private Detective"

4. Tom Selleck _____   d. "Report to Murphy"

5. Clint Eastwood _____   e. "Wonder Woman"

6. Charles Bronson _____   f. "Rockford Files"

7. Mary Tyler Moore _____   g. "Dog and Cat"

8. Nick Nolte _____   h. "Man With a Camera"

9. Patrick Swayze _____   i. "Rawhide"

10. Billy Crystal _____   j. "Soap"

11. Robin Williams _____   k. "Laugh-In"

12. Dennis Weaver _____   l. "Happy Days"

13. Warren Beatty _____   m. "Bosom Buddies"

14. Tom Hanks _____   n. "Gunsmoke"

15. Goldie Hawn _____   o. "St. Elsewhere"

16. Dolly Parton _____   p. "Quest"

17. George C. Scott _____   q. "Sonny and Cher
                               Comedy Hour"

18. Kurt Russell _____
                           r. "Dobie Gillis"
19. Steve Martin _____
                           s. "Porter Wagoner Show"
20. Denzel Washington _____
                           t. "East Side/West Side"
21. Bruce Willis_____
                           u. "Paper Moon"

22. Michelle Pfeiffer _____   v. "B.A.D. Cats"

23. Mia Farrow _____   w. "Peyton Place"

24. Jodie Foster _____   x. "Who Do You Trust?"

25. Lee Marvin _____   y. "Moonlighting"

26. Johnny Carson _____   z. "M Squad"

Test Number 2: THE LONG GOOD-BYE

Now that we've played a little game of "a star is born," we'll fast-forward to those fading stars who turn (or return) to the tube as their light begins to dim. Cruising on "The Love Boat," turning up on "Murder, She Wrote," or embarking as stars or supporting players on soaps or sit-coms, TV is the work stars get (if they're lucky) when their careers begin to slide.

1. This movie golden boy played "Bumper" on a made-for-TV movie adapted from a Joseph Wambaugh novel called *The Blue Knight*. _____

2. One of the biggest box-office stars of the seventies, he now heads the cast of "Evening Shade" and does commercials for Florida orange juice. _____

3. She was America's sweetheart in the early fifties, but she was doing "Hollywood Squares" in the late eighties. Her daughter was Princess Leia. _____

4. He was one of America's most loved actors, but his two attempts at series television both flopped. One of those shows, which ran from 1973 to 1974, was called "Hawkins." His wife's name is Gloria, and he used to recite his poetry on "The Tonight Show." You can hear his off-camera voice on a commercial for Campbell's soup. _____

5. She was a major screen star, was once married to Ronald Reagan, and starred in "Fireside Theatre" for three years in the 1950s. Most recently, she played Angela Channing on "Falcon Crest."

_____

6. Once Jim Anderson's wife, she became Mr. Spock's mother. She was often seen on "The Love Boat" and "St. Elsewhere."

_____

7. He was first seen in a series of Shakespearean plays for what was then NET (National Educational Television), made some good movies, and starred as Mike Hammer, but his talents are now largely wasted as the host of "Missing Reward."

_____

8. These two major stars of the 1940s turned up on "Knots Landing" during the 1984–85 season. They played Paul and Ruth Galveston. In his younger days, he was the husband of Ida Lupino; in her younger days, she was the wife of Mickey Rooney, Artie Shaw, and Frank Sinatra. His name? _____
Her name? _____

9. One of the hottest sex symbols of the 1950s, she turned up on "Falcon Crest" in the 1986–87 season as Kit Marlowe.

_____

10. She was once Archie's daughter, but now you see her on those ads for vocational retraining. _____

Test Number 3: QUITTERS

It's a recurring phenomenon—actors and actresses who establish themselves in a hit series, then quit at the height of the series' success. They quit because of ego, contractual conflicts, boredom, or delusions of grandeur, but when they quit, it makes news, since it disrupts the money-making machine the program has become. We follow these stories because they are always about rising and falling, and there are few stories we like better than that one. We even take sides in the disputes that arise as they prepare to depart. We groan over the temperamental demands of a sitcom star in full pique. They've gotten uppity, we think. Or we think that the networks have been too tightfisted with one of our favorites, though this response is surely less common. In disputes of this kind, we nearly always side with management. There is, perhaps, a small and dark part of ourselves that wishes to see these rapid risers crash and burn, destroy themselves on the sharp edges of their own egos.

In any event, do you remember these famous quitters?

1. She left "Designing Women" because, apparently, no one was treating her right. _____

2. She left "Cheers" for a career in movies. So far, that career has been less than stellar. _____

3. He, the eldest son, left "Bonanza" for more serious work. Shortly thereafter, he was back in a series. _____

4. He was the first in a succession of stars spawned by "Saturday Night Live" who left for the movies. _____

5. She left "Three's Company." Later, she wrote a book about her dysfunctional childhood, and she can be seen doing commercials for Thighmaster. _____

6. He left Mayberry to host his own variety show, but it flopped. Later he turned up on "Three's Company." _____

7. It was the beginning of a legal battle when she left "Charlie's Angels" at the height of her popularity. After several mediocre films, she established her credentials as an actress in a TV movie entitled *The Burning Bed.* _____

8. The actor who played Chester Goode left "Gunsmoke" in 1964, and he's played dozens of TV roles since then. _____

9. This huge "junkyard" hit lost both of its main characters; the father left to do a variety show, the son left when his demands for more money were not met. The father was played by _____ _____ and the son was played by _____ .

10. This show was named for her, but she left after less than one season. Her departure was noisy and acrimonious. Scriptwriters killed her off. The show was renamed "The Hogan Family," and we haven't seen much of her since. _____

Bonus question: Although he wasn't on a series, he is surely the biggest little quitter of them all. He announced an interest in the presidency on "The Larry King Show," withdrew himself from candidacy some months later, then later still, got back in the race—and on nearly every interview show extant._____

Test Number 4: **A BRIEF HISTORY OF ATTITUDE**

"Too big for his britches." That's what my parents' generation said of someone who exhibited an unacceptable degree of smugness, arrogance, vanity, and pride.

In the nineties, it's called "attitude," and it's no longer an entirely bad thing. The word stands on its own now; it no longer requires an adjective. In the nineties, we seldom hear of someone who has a "good" attitude; they just have ATTITUDE, and niceness, cooperation, and fellow feeling have nothing at all to do with it. Tough times call for tough measures, and TV has offered us a host of people we're expected to admire precisely because they make stylish displays of ATTITUDE. The definition of attitude has been expanded to include not only arrogance, but a big dollop of cool, a smidgeon of disdain, a streak of hostility, and a splash of condescension. Self-esteem and self-confidence, so essential to these trying times, gets elevated to the status of ATTITUDE when it crosses the line from passive to aggressive, no matter how mild that aggression might be. And, while we may not like people who display ATTITUDE, we tend to admire them. In the competitive nineties, ATTITUDE is the right stuff.

As in so many other things, TV was into ATTITUDE long before it became fashionable. Showbiz has always been competitive, requiring chutzpah, moxie, and brass of all those who would play the game. It has always attracted people with big egos. The kind of success that comes with TV exposure inflates egos still further.

Some TV personalities are respected or remembered as much for their ATTITUDE as for anything else they do or did. In the test that follows, see what and who you remember in the brief history of ATTITUDE as displayed by television characters or performers. Don't get cocky now; you may not know as much as you think.

The perception of ATTITUDE is a subjective thing, so you'll find my own ATTITUDE all over this test. You may not agree with my assessments, but if the clues give you the correct answer, it's probable that you agree with me.

1. He was known as "the thief of bad gags," and also as "Mr. Television." He was also known for being something of a prima donna. Who?_____

2. He proclaimed himself "The Great One," but we loved him in spite of his outsized ego—or maybe because of it. Who? _____

3. His shtick was based on the character of a neurotic Jewish urbanite, usually talking on the phone. His career went into eclipse after he threw a monumental tantrum captured in a TV documentary called "Comedian Backstage" in 1963.
Who? _____

4. This faded film actress wrote a couple of kiss-and-tell autobiographies in which she claimed to have slept with nearly every male star of her generation (and a generation before and after). She became known for her abrasive personality on the talk shows.
Who? _____

5. This character owns Melville's, the restaurant upstairs from Cheers. He has an abundance of ATTITUDE. What's the character's first name? _____

6. He was a pioneer of the talk show. He wore his emotions close to the surface. He stormed off the show when censors wouldn't let him use the British euphemism for lavatory. Who was that temperamental star? _____

7. We wanted our parents to be like Ward and June, but we would have preferred to be less like Wally and more like his ATTITUDE-ridden friend _____ .

8. From "Saturday Night Live": Fill in the blank.
"I'm _____ , and you're not."

9. The story is that she has thrown temperamental fits over insufficient supplies of bottled water for her daily shampoo. She's one of the twins on "Beverly Hills 90210,"—although maybe not by the time this book comes out. Name the actress._____

10. Cher called him an "asshole," but it was bleeped. Much loved by college students and twentysomethings, he's a late-night master of ATTITUDE. Who's he?_____

11. He's part of the "One-Two-One Club," the support group on "Dear John." He's the abrasive one, played by Jere Burns. Name the character._____

12. When it comes to ATTITUDE, you'd think this guy invented it. His wife, Demi Moore, created a stir when she appeared pregnant and nude on the cover of a national magazine. Who's he?_____

13. Veronica Hamel played her. She was the ultracool public defender and Furillo's love interest on "Hill Street Blues." The character's name?_____

14. If wars can be won on the strength of cockiness, then he won World War II almost single-handedly, though he was being detained by Colonel Klink at the time. Name the character. _____

15. He said skinheads attacked him and marked him with a swastika in a men's room of the San Francisco airport, but reporters thought it was a publicity stunt. Who knows? The guy had ATTITUDE to spare. Who's he?_____

16. He was a speech writer for Agnew and Nixon, but when he's on "Crossfire," he is insufferably mean-spirited and arrogant. He made a failed bid to unseat George Bush in 1992._____

17. He's a giant tub of ATTITUDE. His "ditto-heads" love him, while the "femi-nazis" don't. There's no hurry to name _____ .

18. Smug and smart-assed, he quipped his way through the entire Korean War. His character's name was Hawkeye _____ and the actor who played him (and who often seems pretty self-satisfied himself) is _____ .

19. He played the really gooey lounge singer on "Saturday Night Live," but his public persona as a wise guy is equally redolent of ATTITUDE. He is_____ .

20. He's the radio King of ATTITUDE, the prime "shock jock" of the nation. Name him. _____

21. A James Dean clone of the sixties, he starred in a series called "Then Came Bronson." More recently, he was Jean Reneau on "Twin Peaks." Name him._____

22. When Reagan was shot, this guy rushed on camera to assure everyone that he was "in charge." Many were not reassured. Who's he?_____

23. He doesn't belong in a test about ATTITUDE. When you're in his neighborhood, you talk to Mr. McFeeley, change your shoes, put on a sweater, and you're very, very nice to everyone. Who's he?_____

24. She put out her own best-selling exercise tape, subtitled: "A New Attitude." The ex-mayor of Palm Springs thinks she's had an ATTITUDE right from the start. She is_____ .

25. Dan Aykroyd used to impersonate him on "Saturday Night Live." He hosted a late-night talk show called "Tomorrow" until 1982, and he seemed the essence of self-importance. He is_____ .

Test Number 5: **REMADE FOR TV**

Don't be surprised if you check the TV listings one day to find Luke Perry playing Rhett Butler in a TV movie of *Gone With the Wind.* Or perhaps we can look forward to seeing Bob Saget as Citizen Kane. How about Vanna White as Mrs. Miniver?

You have to wonder why they do it, but they do. They take a classic movie, one we love and remember, and remake it for television. There is no hope of improving on the original. They must know that the critics are going to eat them alive, but still they go on doing it.

See if you can answer the following questions about movies that were remade for television.

Bad Copies

1. It was *the* classic John Ford western, starring John Wayne as Johnny Ringo. When it was remade for TV, Bing Crosby played the dipsomaniac doctor. Nobody remembers anymore who played the Johnny Ringo part. Name the movie._____

2. In the fifties, Patty McCormack played the title role. When this classic was remade in 1985, it starred Blair Brown and David Carradine in this tale of a wicked child.
Can you name the film?_____

3. TV didn't remake it as a movie; it turned it into a *series*. Instead of Humphrey Bogart, it gave us David Soul as Rick Blaine. As compensation, it did offer Scatman Crothers as Sam. Name the classic._____

4. Of all the films he starred in, this was James Stewart's personal favorite. The Frank Capra classic was remade for television with Marlo Thomas in the James Stewart part.
Can you name it? _____

5. She returned to star in a made-for-TV version of the same material, only this time she didn't play Helen Keller; she played what had been Anne Bancroft's part as Helen's teacher. Do you remember her, and the name of the movie?_____

6. It was James Dean's first movie, set in the Salinas Valley and based on a John Steinbeck novel. Jane Seymour, the Queen of TV Movies, starred in this eight-hour epic. Timothy Bottoms played the James Dean role.
Name the movie. _____

7. The original starred Warren Beatty and Natalie Wood in this tale of the horrors of sexual repression. In the made-for-TV version, Melissa Gilbert had the Natalie Wood part, and Michelle Pfeiffer had a smaller role. Do you remember this one?_____

8. It starred the Redgrave sisters, Lynn and Vanessa, and it was that rarity of rarities—a remake that was better than the original. The original starred Bette Davis and Joan Crawford in a minor horror classic. _____

9. The fifties film starred Tony Curtis and Sidney Poitier as escaped convicts. The made-for-TV movie starred Robert Urich and Carl Weathers. Do you know it?_____

10. Gary Cooper on Main Street, Grace Kelly loyally standing by her man. Substitute Lee Majors in the Gary Cooper role, and you have the TV sequel to this classic. _____

1. Debra Winger: **(e) "Wonder Woman"**

2. Michael Keaton: **(d) "Report to Murphy"**

3. Kim Basinger: **(g) "Dog and Cat"**

4. Tom Selleck: **(f) "Rockford Files"**

5. Clint Eastwood: **(i) "Rawhide"**

6. Charles Bronson: **(h) "Man With a Camera"**

7. Mary Tyler Moore: **(c) "Richard Diamond, Private Detective"**

8. Nick Nolte: **(a) "Rich Man, Poor Man"**

9. Patrick Swayze: **(b) "Renegades"**

10. Billy Crystal: **(j) "Soap"**

11. Robin Williams: **(l) "Happy Days"**

12. Dennis Weaver: **(n) "Gunsmoke"**

13. Warren Beatty: **(r) "Dobie Gillis"**

14. Tom Hanks: **(m) "Bosom Buddies"**

15. Goldie Hawn: **(k) "Laugh-In"**

16. Dolly Parton: **(s) "Porter Wagoner Show"**

17. George C. Scott: **(t) "East Side/ West Side"**

Answers

18. Kurt Russell: **(p) "Quest"**

19. Steve Martin: **(q) "Sonny and Cher Comedy Hour"**

20. Denzel Washington: **(o) "St. Elsewhere"**

21. Bruce Willis: **(y) "Moonlighting"**

22. Michelle Pfeiffer: **(v) "B.A.D. Cats"**

23. Mia Farrow: **(w) "Peyton Place"**

24. Jodie Foster: **(u) "Paper Moon"**

25. Lee Marvin: **(z) "M Squad"**

26. Johnny Carson: **(x) "Who Do You Trust?"**

Test Number 2: **THE LONG GOOD-BYE**

1. **William Holden** played "Bumper" in "The Blue Knight."

2. **Burt Reynolds** stars in "Evening Shade" and does commercials for Florida orange juice.

3. America's sweetheart in the early fifties who appeared on "Hollywood Squares" in the eighties was **Debbie Reynolds**.

4. **Jimmy Stewart** was the well-loved film actor who never quite made it on TV.

5. Ronald Reagan's ex-wife who played Angela Channing on "Falcon Crest" was **Jane Wyman**.

6. Jim Anderson's wife, Margaret, was played by **Jane Wyatt**.

7. **Stacy Keach** starred as Mike Hammer, but his talents are now largely wasted as the host of "Missing Reward."

8. Paul and Ruth Galveston were played by **Howard Duff** and **Ava Gardner**.

9. Kit Marlowe was played by **Kim Novak**.

10. Once known for her role as Gloria on "All in the Family," **Sally Struthers** now does ads for vocational retraining.

Test Number 3: QUITTERS

1. She left "Designing Women" because, apparently, no one was treating her right: **Delta Burke**

2. She left "Cheers" for a career in movies. So far, that career has been less than stellar: **Shelley Long**

3. He, the eldest son, left "Bonanza" for more serious work. Shortly thereafter, he was back in a series: **Pernell Roberts**

4. He was the first in a succession of stars spawned by "Saturday Night Live" who left for the movies, then crashed on late-night: **Chevy Chase**

5. She left "Three's Company." Later, she wrote a book about her dysfunctional childhood, and she can be seen doing commercials for Thighmaster: **Suzanne Somers**

6. He left Mayberry to host his own variety show, but it flopped. Later he turned up on "Three's Company": **Don Knotts**

7. It was the beginning of a legal battle when she left "Charlie's Angels" at the height of her popularity. After several mediocre films, she established her credentials as an actress in a TV movie entitled *The Burning Bed:* **Farrah Fawcett**

8. The actor who played Chester Goode left "Gunsmoke" in 1964, and he's played dozens of TV roles since then: **Dennis Weaver**

9. This huge "junkyard" hit lost both of its main characters. The father was played by **Redd Foxx** and the son was played by **Demond Wilson.**

10. This show was named for her, but she left after less than one season. Scriptwriters killed her off. The show was renamed "The Hogan Family," and we haven't seen much of her since: **Valerie Harper**

Bonus question: The biggest little quitter of them all: **Ross Perot**

Test Number 4: **A BRIEF HISTORY OF ATTITUDE**

1. "Mr. Television": **Milton Berle**

2. "The Great One": **Jackie Gleason**

3. "Comedian Backstage": **Shelley Berman**

4. She claimed to have slept with nearly every male star of her generation: **Shelley Winters**

5. Melville's owner's first name is **John.**

6. The talk show pioneer who wore his emotions close to the surface was **Jack Paar**.

7. Wally's ATTITUDE-ridden friend was **Eddie Haskell**.

8. "I'm **Chevy Chase,** and you're not."

9. The temperamental twin is **Shannen Doherty**.

10. Cher called him an "asshole": **David Letterman**

11. Jere Burns plays the abrasive **Kirk Morris**.

12. Demi's husband: **Bruce Willis**

13. Veronica Hamel played the ultracool **Joyce Davenport**.

14. Detained by Colonel Klink at the time: **Colonel Robert Hogan**

15. Skinheads attacked him in a men's room of the San Francisco airport, maybe: **Morton Downey, Jr.**

16. Arrogant and mean-spirited former cohost of "Crossfire": **Pat Buchanan**

17. He's a giant tub of ATTITUDE. His "ditto-heads" love him: **Rush Limbaugh**

18. Smug and smart-assed, he quipped his way through the entire Korean War: Hawkeye **Pierce/Alan Alda**

19. He played the really gooey lounge singer on "Saturday Night Live": **Bill Murray**

20. The number one radio jock and king of ATTITUDE: **Howard Stern**

21. He starred in "Then Came Bronson": **Michael Parks**

22. When Reagan was shot, this guy rushed on camera to assure everyone that he was "in charge": **Alexander Haig**

23. When you're in his neighborhood, you talk to Mr. McFeeley: **Mr. Fred Rogers**

24. She put out her own best-selling exercise tape, subtitled: "A New Attitude": **Cher**

25. Dan Aykroyd used to impersonate him on "Saturday Night Live": **Tom Snyder**

Test Number 5: **REMADE FOR TV**

1. It was *the* classic John Ford western, starring John Wayne and remade for TV: *Stagecoach*

2. It starred Blair Brown and David Carradine in a tale of a wicked child: *The Bad Seed*

3. David Soul as Rick Blaine? The remade classic: *Casablanca*

4. The Frank Capra classic remade for television with Marlo Thomas: *It's a Wonderful Life*

5. She played what had been Anne Bancroft's part as Helen's teacher. She is **Patty Duke**, and the movie is *The Miracle Worker*.

6. James Dean's first movie and the miniseries remake: ***East of Eden***

7. In the made-for-TV version, Melissa Gilbert had the Natalie Wood part: ***Splendor in the Grass***

8. It starred the Redgrave sisters, Lynn and Vanessa, and it was that rarity of rarities—a remake that was better than the original: ***What Ever Happened to Baby Jane?***

9. The made-for-TV movie starred Robert Urich and Carl Weathers. It was: ***The Defiant Ones***

10. Gary Cooper on Main Street, Grace Kelly loyally standing by her man: ***High Noon***

This test has a bit of an attitude itself. I hope that won't throw off your ability to discern the answers to the questions.

There are 82 questions in this sequence. Even if you disagreed with the point of view expressed, you probably remembered the people under discussion, at least in many of the questions.

Scoring

> **62–82 Correct: Showbiz savvy.**
>
> **40–61 Correct: They catch your inter-est, but don't always hold it.**
>
> **0–39 Correct: You could care less about this stuff, and you're probably a better person for that.**

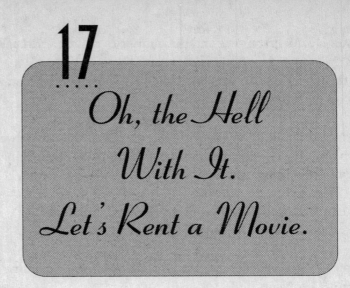

17

Oh, the Hell With It. Let's Rent a Movie.

"The words 'Kiss Kiss, Bang Bang,' which I saw on an Italian movie poster, are perhaps the briefest statement imaginable of the basic appeal of movies."

PAULINE KAEL

By now, you may be pretty sick of TV. It's time to rent a movie. More people see movies on television than in the theaters.

Listen to people talking in video stores. They may know a great deal about movies, but they have trouble remembering titles. "Let's get that one—I forget the name—about a dog."

In the next test, imagine you are listening to people trying to find movies in the video store. Can you help them? If so, provide the title of the movie they're looking for.

1. "It's the movie about a nuclear power plant accident. Jack Lemmon overacts." _____

2. "It's that one with Rick Moranis where the kids are all tiny." _____

3. "You know—the one about two women who kill a redneck and take off in a T-Bird." _____

4. "It's got Cher, and she's got a deformed kid." _____

5. "The one about the guy who comes back from the future to kill people."_____

6. "Kevin Costner and Indians." _____

7. "Kevin Costner and Whitney Houston." _____

8. "Her boyfriend dies, you know, and then comes back to help her out." _____

9. "Hippies on Harleys." _____

10. "Yuppies on coke, with Michael J. Fox." _____

11. "It's about that labor guy who disappeared." _____

12. "Starts with an A, about a genie." _____

13. "The first one with Freddy Krueger in it." _____

14. "You know, it's got that wild and crazy guy in it, and he plays a preacher." _____

Oh, the Hell With It. Let's Rent a Movie.

15. "It's based on a book by James Fenimore Cooper. That English guy's in it . . . Daniel Day-Lewis."_____

16. "Michael Caine and the Muppets."_____

17. "It's the one where Elvis dies at the end."_____

18. "There's a sled in it named 'Rosebud.'"_____

19. "Robert Duvall says, 'I love the smell of napalm in the morning.'"
_____

20. "Dustin Hoffman has an affair with his girlfriend's mom."
_____

21. "That guy who used to play Jim on 'Taxi' is in it, and he's this crazy scientist with a DeLorean."_____

22. "Richard Dreyfuss makes a mountain out of mashed potatoes."
_____

23. "There's this St. Bernard, and he makes a mess of everything."
_____

24. "It was John Wayne's last movie, and he's this guy who's dying of cancer."_____

25. "You know the one: Marlon Brando's got cotton in his cheeks."
_____

26. "It's a prostitute who gets picked up by this rich guy played by Richard Gere, and they fall in love."
_____

27. "Madonna plays a baseball player."_____

28. "It's got this guy Jason who wears, like, a hockey mask." _____

29. "Paul Newman is this pool shark, and he goes up against Jackie Gleason." _____

30. "This big ape trashes New York. You know the one."_____

31. "Charlton Heston has this big chariot race scene."_____

32. "This yuppie couple hire a nanny, and she's crazy."_____

33. "It's got Nick Nolte and Eddie Murphy. One of them's a cop, and the other's a convict." _____

34. "Kirk Douglas is like a gladiator or something." _____

35. "There's this English dude who dresses up like an Arab and rides a camel." _____

36. "Warren Beatty plays a gangster who invents Las Vegas." _____

37. "It's Errol Flynn in the woods with a bunch of Merry Men." _____

38. "This fat guy runs all over trying to talk to the head of General Motors." _____

39. "Dustin Hoffman gets his teeth drilled by this Nazi doctor— and no novocaine." _____

40. "Burt Reynolds wears these funky seventies clothes and gets chased all over by Jackie Gleason." _____

41. "Paul Newman and Robert Redford get killed by the whole Bolivian army." _____

42. "Humphrey Bogart's a drunk, and Katharine Hepburn is this uptight lady, and they're on a boat." _____

43. "This guy dresses up as his own mother and kills a lady in the shower." _____

44. "It's two cops, and one doesn't care whether he lives or dies so he's real reckless." _____

45. "It was a real bomb—with Bruce Willis as a thief." _____

46. "Tom Cruise plays this marine lawyer who goes after Jack Nicholson." _____

47. "It's about this dad and his two sons fishing up in Montana."

_____

48. "This family goes off to Paris, but they forget one of their kids."

_____

49. "It's about these preppies, and Robin Williams is their English teacher, and one commits suicide." _____

50. "Marlon Brando is always yelling for Stella." _____

51. "A bunch of guys with mid-life crisis go on a cattle drive."

_____

52. "This kid's parents go away, and he starts a brothel while they're gone." _____

53. "Shirley MacLaine's the mom, and Debra Winger's the daughter, and Debra Winger dies." _____

54. "Humphrey Bogart runs this cafe, but he's never gotten over Ingrid Bergman." _____

55. "James Dean plays this poor guy who strikes it rich in Texas oil." _____

56. "There are these two guys on the run from gangsters, so they disguise themselves as women musicians." _____

57. "It's the movie where Elizabeth Taylor met Richard Burton and dumped Eddie Fisher." _____

58. "These Okies all head for California during the Depression. Henry Fonda's in it." _____

59. "You know, the one where the guy has a big rabbit for a friend, but only he can see it." _____

60. "The commies program this guy so he'll kill the president, but Frank Sinatra saves the day." _____

61. "Sean Connery is a submarine captain trying to defect from the Soviet Union, back when there was one."

_____

62. "It's about this weird overgrown kid and his bicycle."

_____

63. "These two dudes do a TV show in their basement."

_____

64. "This hotshot Hollywood producer kills a screenwriter."

_____

65. "That Shakespeare guy wrote it. Mel Gibson's in it."

_____

Oh, the Hell With It. Let's Rent a Movie.

66. "Robert De Niro's this wacko who saves Jodie Foster from a life of prostitution." _____

67. "Jodie Foster's this FBI agent tracking down a serial killer." _____

68. "Kathleen Turner writes romance novels, but she gets involved with Michael Douglas in South America." _____

69. "You know, the one where Jon Voight goes to New York and meets Ratso Rizzo." _____

70. "Michael Caine is married to Mia Farrow, but he's in love with her sister." _____

71. "Dean Martin and Jerry Lewis are paratroopers." _____

72. "David Niven and that Mexican actor, Cantinflas, in a big Mike Todd production." _____

73. "Jack Nicholson plays a hit man. He falls in love with Kathleen Turner, and she's a hit man, too." _____

74. "This Vietnam vet gets hassled by the cops, so he wipes everybody out." _____

75. "James Spader is this guy with a video camera who gets everyone to tell their fantasies on tape." _____

76. "The one where Sharon Stone crosses her legs, and she's not wearing underpants." _____

77. "Doris Day and Rock Hudson do a lot of flirting over the phone." _____

78. "These rival gangs—the Jets, and I forget the other one—are going to have a rumble, but first they all dance." _____

79. "Barbra Streisand is this upscale New York shrink, and Nick Nolte teaches her son to play football." _____

80. "There's this bitchin' scene where Warren Beatty and Faye Dunaway get blown away by about a zillion bullets."

   _____

81. "It's the only movie James Taylor ever made. Warren Oates is in it." _____

82. "Jane Fonda falls in love with this guy in a wheelchair, and her husband gets back from Vietnam and commits suicide."

   _____

83. "Al Pacino kills Sterling Hayden in a restaurant."

   _____

84. "You know, it was the Beatles' first movie." _____

85. "The U2 movie. I can't remember the name." _____

86. "Guns n' Roses wrote the music. Emilio Estevez plays Billy the Kid." _____

87. "Madonna's documentary where she makes fun of Kevin Costner." _____

88. "This French guy is trying to get papers so he can work, so he pretends to marry Andie MacDowell." _____

89. "Spike Lee works in this pizza joint, but then there's trouble in the 'hood." _____

Oh, the Hell With It. Let's Rent a Movie.

90. "Clark Gable tries to round up wild horses for slaughter, but Marilyn Monroe stops him." _____

91. "The head of this savings and loan outfit tries to kill himself on Christmas Eve." _____

92. "It's all about disco dancing, and who's the best dancer. John Travolta was in it." _____

93. "It's all about riding mechanical bulls, and who's the best at it. John Travolta's in it." _____

94. "It's about this washed-up rodeo rider who steals a horse from Las Vegas." _____

95. "This crazy lady saves a writer from a wreck in the snow, then she keeps him prisoner." _____

96. "Robin Williams is this nerdy doctor, and Robert De Niro is his patient." _____

97. "Meg Ryan has that big scene where she fakes an orgasm in a restaurant." _____

98. "Richard Gere carries Debra Winger out of the factory where she works. Everybody claps." _____

99. "A widow works to harvest her cotton crop so she won't lose the farm." _____

100. "Charles Bronson turns vigilante after his wife and daughter are raped and murdered." _____

1. It's the movie about a nuclear power plant accident: *The China Syndrome*

2. It's that one with Rick Moranis: *Honey, I Shrunk the Kids*

3. Two women kill a redneck and take off in a T-Bird: *Thelma and Louise*

4. Cher's got a deformed kid: *Mask*

5. The guy comes back from the future to kill people: *The Terminator*

6. Kevin Costner and Indians: *Dances With Wolves*

7. Kevin Costner and Whitney Houston: *The Bodyguard*

8. Her boyfriend dies, you know, and then comes back to help her out: *Ghost*

9. Hippies on Harleys: *Easy Rider*

10. Yuppies on coke, with Michael J. Fox: *Bright Lights, Big City*

11. That labor guy who disappeared: *Hoffa*

12. Starts with an A, about a genie: *Aladdin*

13. The first one with Freddy Krueger: *A Nightmare on Elm Street*

14. It's got that wild and crazy guy in it, and he plays a preacher: *Leap of Faith*

15. Based on a book by James Fenimore Cooper: *The Last of the Mohicans*

Oh, the Hell With It. Let's Rent a Movie.

Answers

16. Michael Caine and the Muppets: *A Muppet Christmas Carol*

17. Elvis dies at the end: *Love Me Tender*

18. A sled named "Rosebud": *Citizen Kane*

19. "I love the smell of napalm in the morning": *Apocalypse Now*

20. Dustin Hoffman's affair with his girlfriend's mom: *The Graduate*

21. Jim on "Taxi" is this crazy scientist with a DeLorean: *Back to the Future*

22. Richard Dreyfuss makes a mountain out of mashed potatoes: *Close Encounters of the Third Kind*

23. This St. Bernard makes a mess of everything: *Beethoven*

24. John Wayne's last movie: *The Shootist*

25. Marlon Brando's got cotton in his cheeks: *The Godfather*

26. A prostitute gets picked up by a rich guy played by Richard Gere: *Pretty Woman*

27. Madonna plays a baseball player: *A League of Their Own*

28. This guy Jason wears a hockey mask: *Halloween*

29. Paul Newman goes up against Jackie Gleason: *The Hustler*

30. This big ape trashes New York: *King Kong*

31. Charlton Heston has this big chariot race: *Ben-Hur*

32. Yuppie couple hire a crazy nanny: *The Hand That Rocks the Cradle*

33. Nick Nolte and Eddie Murphy: *48 Hours*

34. Kirk Douglas is a gladiator: *Spartacus*

35. English dude dresses up like a sheikh, rides camel: *Lawrence of Arabia*

Answers

36. Warren Beatty, a gangster who invents Las Vegas: *Bugsy*

37. Errol Flynn in the woods: *The Adventures of Robin Hood*

38. This fat guy runs all over trying to talk to the head of General Motors: *Roger and Me*

39. Dustin Hoffman gets his teeth drilled: *Marathon Man*

40. Burt Reynolds gets chased by Jackie Gleason: *Smokey and the Bandit*

41. Paul Newman and Robert Redford get killed: *Butch Cassidy and the Sundance Kid*

42. Humphrey Bogart and Katharine Hepburn on a boat: *The African Queen*

43. This guy kills a lady in the shower: *Psycho*

44. Two cops; one doesn't care whether he lives or dies: *Lethal Weapon*

45. A bomb. Bruce Willis as a thief: *Hudson Hawk*

46. Tom Cruise goes after Jack Nicholson: *A Few Good Men*

47. This dad and his two sons go fishing up in Montana: *A River Runs Through It*

Oh, the Hell With It. Let's Rent a Movie.

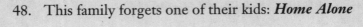
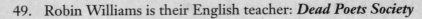

48. This family forgets one of their kids: **Home Alone**

49. Robin Williams is their English teacher: **Dead Poets Society**

50. Marlon Brando yelling for Stella: **A Streetcar Named Desire**

51. Guys with mid-life crisis on a cattle drive: **City Slickers**

52. Kid starts a brothel while his parents are gone: **Risky Business**

53. Shirley MacLaine's the mom, and Debra Winger dies: **Terms of Endearment**

54. Humphrey Bogart's never gotten over Ingrid Bergman: **Casablanca**

55. James Dean plays "Strike It Rich" in Texas oil: **Giant**

56. Two guys on the run disguise themselves as women: **Some Like It Hot**

57. Elizabeth Taylor met Richard Burton and dumped Eddie Fisher: **Cleopatra**

58. Okies head for California during the Depression: **The Grapes of Wrath**

59. The guy has a big rabbit for a friend: **Harvey**

60. Commies program this guy so he'll kill the president: **The Manchurian Candidate**

61. Sean Connery tries to defect from the Soviet Union: **The Hunt for Red October**

62. Weird overgrown kid and his bicycle: **Pee Wee's Big Adventure**

63. Two dudes do a TV show in their basement: *Wayne's World*

64. Hollywood producer kills a screenwriter: *The Player*

65. Shakespeare wrote it. Mel Gibson's in it: *Hamlet*

66. Robert De Niro saves Jodie Foster: *Taxi Driver*

67. Jodie Foster tracks down a serial killer: *Silence of the Lambs*

68. Kathleen Turner gets involved with Michael Douglas in South America: *Romancing the Stone*

69. Jon Voight goes to New York and meets Ratso Rizzo: *Midnight Cowboy*

70. Michael Caine's in love with Mia's sister: *Hannah and Her Sisters*

71. Dean Martin and Jerry Lewis are paratroopers: *Jumping Jacks*

72. David Niven in a big Mike Todd production: *Around the World in Eighty Days*

73. Jack Nicholson falls in love with Kathleen Turner: *Prizzi's Honor*

74. Vietnam vet gets hassled by the cops, wipes everybody out: *Rambo*

75. Everyone tells their fantasies on tape: *sex, lies, and videotape*

76. Sharon Stone crosses her legs, and she's not wearing underpants: *Basic Instinct*

77. Doris Day and Rock Hudson flirt over the phone: *Pillow Talk*

Oh, the Hell With It. Let's Rent a Movie.

78. Rival gangs dance: ***West Side Story***

79. Barbra Streisand and Nick Nolte: ***Prince of Tides***

80. Warren Beatty and Faye Dunaway get blown away: ***Bonnie and Clyde***

81. The only movie James Taylor ever made: ***Two-Lane Blacktop***

82. Jane Fonda falls in love with this guy in a wheelchair: ***Coming Home***

83. Al Pacino kills Sterling Hayden in a restaurant: ***The Godfather***

84. The Beatles' first movie: ***A Hard Day's Night***

85. The U2 movie: ***Rattle and Hum***

86. Guns n' Roses wrote the music: ***Young Guns***

87. Madonna's documentary: ***Truth or Dare***

88. French guy trying to get papers: ***Green Card***

89. Spike Lee works in this pizza joint: ***Do the Right Thing***

90. Clark Gable tries to round up wild horses: ***The Misfits***

91. Savings and loan head tries to kill himself on Christmas Eve: ***It's a Wonderful Life***

92. John Travolta, about disco dancing: ***Saturday Night Fever***

93. John Travolta, about riding mechanical bulls: ***Urban Cowboy***

94. Rodeo rider steals a horse from Vegas: ***Electric Horseman***

95. Crazy lady saves a writer, then keeps him prisoner: *Misery*

96. Robin Williams, doctor; Robert De Niro, patient: *Awakenings*

97. Meg Ryan fakes an orgasm: *When Harry Met Sally*

98. Richard Gere/Debra Winger. Everybody claps: *An Officer and a Gentleman*

99. Widow harvests her cotton crop: *Places in the Heart*

100. Charles Bronson turns vigilante after his wife and daughter are raped and murdered: *Death Wish*

There are many times more video stores in America than there are libraries. You can always find a video store open, but seldom can you find a library open. If you're one of that legion of people who rent movies all the time, then you probably knew most of the answers to the questions on this test. Check it out.

Scoring

80–100 Correct: Two thumbs up.

50–79 Correct: Can't recommend.

0–49 Correct: Culturally deprived, or perhaps you've been reading.

Oh, the Hell With It. Let's Rent a Movie.

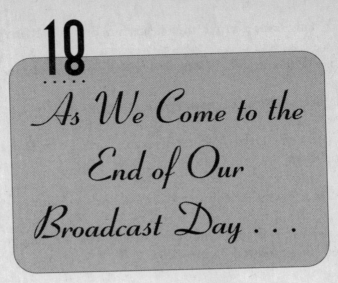

18

As We Come to the End of Our Broadcast Day . . .

The wee hours are upon us. Letterman is long gone. Even Bob Costas has bid us farewell. Now we are in the land of water bed commercials and old movies. We sit channel surfing with the remote, looking for a culminating event, some last good thing to see before going off to bed. Perhaps we are at that stage of tiredness where we cannot quite muster the energy to go to bed, so we work the remote in search of something bad enough to motivate us from the living room to the bedroom, something that will make us punch the power button to "off," the television light dimming slowly enough so that we can make our way by its fading light all the way to the hall.

Across America, most people are asleep, but in New York and in Los

Angeles an army of people is already scurrying about to prepare our early morning viewing menu. Guests for the early morning talk shows are pacing hotel rooms, changing ties, waiting for the limos that will pick them up. Actors and actresses are readying themselves for the drive to the studio, to the daily routine of makeup and script run-throughs. Meteorologists are checking in with the National Weather Service. News anchors are checking the wire services for stories that developed while half the world slept. Jay Leno is finishing up his day, working with his writers on jokes for the next night's monologue. Advertising people awake from sleep to jot ideas for campaigns or slogans on a pad they keep on the nightstand. Producers and production assistants have already taken up the myriad worries that will preoccupy them for much of the coming day.

We slip into our beds, concerned that we will be tired on the job, that the tube and our own inertia have kept us up too late. It is only a few hours from the time we will be sharing coffee with Bryant, Katie, and Willard, or doing morning exercises with Jake or Richard. We will be getting an idea of the traffic that faces us from the local broadcasts that punctuate "Today," "Good Morning America," and "CBS This Morning." We'll choose what to wear based on the man or woman who stands in front of a busy map, cheerfully forecasting whatever weather is headed our way. The toothpaste we cleanse our teeth with, the soap we cleanse our bodies with, the foam we shave our faces with, the cereal we eat, the clothes we don, the fragrances we spray on ourselves, the car we will drive to work—all have been selected through the persuasive force of our viewing. And, as our wavering attention returns to the images and sounds of the morning broadcasts, our concerns and our latent fears will be awakened about terrible things happening in faraway places, and sometimes near to home; the world will come rushing back into our fuzzy consciousness once more.

But for now we leave it behind—the world as it is, and the world as television has given us to know it. We settle beneath the blankets, in search of dreams, the little teleplays where we ourselves always have the starring roles.